Live. Learn. Laugh!

*Stories and studies that reveal
God's amazing heart*

by Mary Ann Crum

PRESS

www.xulonpress.com

Contents

Lost to found ... aimless to anchored ...
doomed to delivered.
Let's talk about ...

SALVATION

A Male Who Can Find What's Lost

They say that as married couples grow older, they start to become more and more alike — a prospect that probably terrifies my husband even more than it does me. I'm beginning to think "they" might be right.

For example, when I was recently in a shop looking for an air freshener thing for my car, I wandered through the whole store but couldn't find what I was looking for. An observant saleslady asked if I needed some help.

"I'm looking for a citrus and sage air freshener," I said.

"It's right here," she said, plucking it off a hook a few inches from me and directly in my line of sight.

"How did I not see that?" I stammered.

And then it dawned on me — the morphing-into-your spouse thing.

"Oh, no," I groaned, sounding like I had just looked in the mirror and realized I was growing a rhino horn. "This is AWFUL. My husband and sons can't find anything in our house and now I ... I'm becoming just like THEM."

(Cue scary organ music.)

This was serious. After all, what household can survive if the woman loses her ability to find stuff?

Okay, ladies, tell me I'm not alone in my frustration and astonishment that roughly half the human race — the male half — usually can't find anything once it is put into a cabinet, closet, drawer or refrigerator.

Think I'm making this up? Unh-uh.

We were eating dinner the other night and I was glad to finally sit down after an exhausting afternoon. I had just parked my hind-quarters on a chair when my husband went to the refrigerator to search for salad dressing.

"Might as well get it for him—he'll never find it," I thought.

"Oh, surely he'll see it," another part of my brain countered.

I heard bottles clinking, plastic thumping, and aluminum foil rustling as my husband rooted through the nether regions of the fridge.

"We don't have any salad dressing," he said.

"Yeah, we do—it's right there on the door," I responded, "... where it always is." (I couldn't resist.)

"No, I don't see it. We must not have any."

"Yeah, really, we do. It's on the door. I'll get it."

I hoisted myself out of my chair and clump ... clump ... clumped over to the fridge, where I located the salad dressing in about a nanosecond.

I shook my head ever so slightly for dramatic effect and mar-veled to myself, "How in the world does this man solve complex computer problems every day?" as I clump ... clump ... clumped back to the table.

"Well ... the bottle was turned around backwards and I couldn't read the label," he said.

If you feel I'm unfairly picking on my mate over a rare and isolated incident, let me say a big fat, "I don't think so." Variations of the salad-dressing scene have been played out in my house so many times that I'm poised to spring into search-and-rescue mode any time my husband or sons reach for the pantry door or refrigerator handle. I am the designated finder of all that is allegedly, but not really, lost.

Please don't misunderstand my gentle jabbing here—I'm not a male-bashing "femiNazi." I love my guys. And I certainly have no problem with all the references to God that are male in nature—Father, Son, Lord, and King, for example. In fact, I find much comfort in those descriptions of God.

I know that God embodies all that is good and perfect about both males and females, but because I tend to think of God in masculine terms, and because I tend to assume that some men are ... um ... challenged when it comes to finding stuff, I catch myself being shamefully surprised at how good God is at finding lost things, particularly people who've lost their way in life.

Like me.

"I once was lost, but now am found." A miracle anyway you look at it.

Doing the Walmart Waltz

Okay, raise your hand if you've ever come out of Walmart and forgotten where your car is parked.

C'mon, raise 'em high. I've seen you. In fact, I've been you.

What is it about that parking lot? No matter how hard I try to remember where my car is, I always seem to emerge from Walmart befuddled. Going in, I consciously note that my car is lined up with the big "W" or the little "t" on the sign, but by the time I'm ready to leave, my neurotransmitters have usually sputtered out.

And so begins the Walmart Waltz, as I weave and glide around the lot with my cart looking for my silver Toyota. It's small consolation that I'm rarely alone on the dance floor.

I think the parking lot rows used to be numbered, but not anymore. I suspect the numbers were removed so that employees can watch surveillance videos and mock goofballs like me.

I'm not sure what the parking situation is like at Disney World these days, but the last time we were there, I appreciated how relatively easy it was to find our car. It's a good thing or my family would probably still be wandering around the fringes of the Magic Kingdom. The Disney lots were named after characters and each row had a number. We only had to remember "Goofy 3" or "Pluto 9" and we were set.

It's not so easy at Walmart.

It doesn't help that something about that store thoroughly drains my brain. Maybe it's dodging the turbocharged seniors cruising the aisles on shopping scooters; or hiking 10 miles because my shopping list isn't efficiently organized; or running into every friend who lives within a three-county radius; or being rebuked by the self-scanning checkout robot who loudly, repeatedly, and wrongly accuses me of not bagging all my items.

Wait, that reminds me of something. Can I digress for a moment here? I want to explain why I often use the self-checkout line. It's not relevant, but I want to explain: It's because as a child, I thought that being a grocery store checkout lady would be the coolest job ever. Before scanners were invented, checkout ladies had to have fingers as speedy and nimble as brain surgeons. It seemed like a high calling.

Alas, my career path never included operating a cash register, so self-checkout lines are as close as I get to my childhood dream job.

But back to my point: The whole Walmart experience generally renders my brain so numb that when I emerge from the store, I scarcely know what planet I'm on, let alone where my car is parked.

"Let's see ... was it by the garden center or the groceries? Was my parking space slanted in towards the store or away from it? Does moss grow on the north side of light posts? If I just stay where I am, will somebody eventually find me out here?"

Forget about it—I'm lost and all I can do is start roaming and searching. The waltz begins.

You know, some people wander through life the way I wander through the Walmart parking lot. They wander and wonder, "What am I here for? Where am I going? What's true?"

They line themselves up with something, or anything, to get their bearings—money, social status, professional success, sensual pleasure.

But when crises occur (and they always do), that "thing" they've used for direction and purpose is no help at all.

I've been there, done that, and it's a bad feeling. Then I lined myself up with just one thing, one Person—Jesus Christ—and my wandering days were over.

I've been lost, and I've been found ... and found is a whole lot better. At Walmart, but even more in life.

"Keep your eyes on Jesus, who both began and finished this race we're in." – Hebrews 12:2a (The Message)

As Helpless as a Fish in the Woods

A bass stranded in a drainage ditch, a couple of ladies on their way to a party, dense woods and a nearby pond—perhaps not a typical setting for an epic rescue story ... and yet, it was ... sort of.

Some women from my church were getting together for an event at a friend's home, and as the ladies were arriving, the hostess looked out her back window and said, "What in the world are they doing out there?"

We gathered around the window and saw two of our friends in the woods, obviously trying to catch something. Theories abounded.

"It's probably a lizard," I said, knowing that one of the ladies has a special affinity (I'm not kidding) for lizards.

"I bet it's a kitten," someone else said. "You know Beth can't resist saving kittens."

About that time, we watched one of the gals emerge from the dense woods clutching—get this—a big fish.

"Look! Heidi caught a bass in the woods!" I announced.

Beth and Heidi took off running toward the pond, and when they reached the shore, Heidi shot-putted the fish into the water, where he swam away and was, undoubtedly, as relieved and thankful as a bass can be.

Smelling a bit fishy all evening was the price Heidi paid for her heroics, but according to her, it was worth it.

Heidi explained that as she and Beth were walking toward the house, they heard something flopping around in a shallow drainage ditch that ran from a goldfish pond, past the woods and down to the big pond out back. Tenderhearted, animal-loving Beth first saw the hapless bass but was a bit freaked out about just grabbing it.

"He's gonna die if we just leave him here," she said to Heidi, who happened to be walking alongside her.

"Here, hold my cupcakes and I'll get him," Heidi said. And that's just what she did. Once she nabbed the flailing fish, both ladies took off running toward the pond, but after just a few steps, the slimy bass rallied for one final burst and leapt out of Heidi's grasp and into the woods.

Pondering whether they wanted to risk chiggers and ticks to save the fish, Heidi said she thought, "Oh, great—he might have lived if I'd left him in the ditch, but he's gonna die for sure in those woods." So she went in after him.

Ever tried to catch a desperate, flopping fish in thick brush? Me either, but I'm pretty sure it's not anyone's idea of a good time. But Heidi and Beth did it and there is one more bass in the world today because of their heroics.

The whole escapade was good for some laughs, but it also seemed like a pretty good picture of another rescue mission of infinitely greater importance that took place 2,000 years ago. A loving God saw His favorite creatures doomed and helpless in a hostile environment, so He ventured into the thick mess to rescue us. He ended up with much more than chigger bites and ticks for his heroics—He was rejected, humiliated, tortured and crucified.

Are you thinking you don't need to be rescued?

Make no mistake—no matter how together we may look on the outside, if our hearts are separated from Jesus Christ, we're all as helpless and doomed as ... well ... a fish in the woods.

Let's Talk About Salvation ... Group Discussion Questions

1. As you reflect upon your life, do you have a sense that God ever came looking for you?

2. What are some examples in the Bible of people who were sought and found by God? (A few hints to get you started: think burning bush, belly of a whale, blinding light on a road, wee little man, and fishers of men.)

3. Is it difficult or easy for you to believe that God would search for you if you lose your way in life?

4. Money, social status, professional success and sensual pleasure were mentioned as things people sometimes try to use as a compass to get their bearings in life. In Matthew 7:24-27, we find a parable Jesus told on a similar theme. What was the message Jesus was trying to communicate? How does the message of this parable relate to salvation?

5. Read Ephesians 2:8-9 and Titus 3:3-7. What support do these verses lend to the proposition that we are as "helpless as a bass in the woods" without God? What makes that truth so hard for many people to accept?

6. Can you think of any Scriptures that describe or reveal God's heart toward us and explain why He would care whether or not we have lost our way?

7. Read Luke 15:1-10. In these two parables, what is the reaction of the owners of the sheep and the coin when they find what was lost? What is the reaction in heaven when one sinner repents?

What was Jesus trying to show us in these verses about the heart of God?

8. What are some ways we can participate in God's plan to rescue people who are lost?

9. Has God ever used you as part of His rescue mission in someone else's life?

10. Have each person in the group pray (silently or out loud) to be part of God's rescue mission in the life of a specific, unbelieving family member, friend, coworker or acquaintance.

Dig a Little Deeper ... Individual Study Questions

1. Read Luke 15:4-7 -- *"What man among you, if he has a hundred sheep and has lost one of them, does not leave the ninety-nine in the open pasture and go after the one which is lost until he finds it? When he has found it, he lays it on his shoulders, rejoicing. And when he comes home, he calls together his friends and his neighbors, saying to them, 'Rejoice with me, for I have found my sheep which was lost!' I tell you that in the same way, there will be more joy in heaven over one sinner who repents than over ninety-nine righteous persons who need no repentance."*

   - Jesus told this parable in response to criticism He received from the Pharisees because He spent time with sinners and tax-collectors. Answer the following questions about this passage:

- Who do the sheep represent in this parable? _____

_____

- Who does the shepherd represent? _____

_____

- If you're a Christian, then you realize that Jesus, the Good Shepherd, found you when you were lost. Briefly describe how and when that happened: _____

_____

_____

_____

_____

2. Read John 10:14 – "*I am the good shepherd, and I know My own and My own know Me.*"

- Now go back to the parable of the lost sheep in Luke 15:4-7, bearing in mind that Jesus is the Shepherd in this verse and we are His "sheep." According to Jesus' parable, what will He do if you stray from Him? _____

_____

_____

- How does that make you feel? (loved, secure, guilty, paranoid?) Explain: _____

_____

_____

_____

- According to the parable, what does the shepherd (Jesus) do with the lost sheep when He finds it? _____

  _____

- What does the shepherd (Jesus) do when He returns home with His rescued sheep? _____

  _____

3. If you are a believer in Christ, can you recall a time, even as a Christian, when you strayed from God and He came searching for you? _____ What were the circumstances? _____

   _____

   _____

   _____

   _____

   _____

   _____

4. Now read these verses from other parables Jesus told on this subject:

   - Luke 15:8-10 – *"Or what woman, if she has ten silver coins and loses one coin, does not light a lamp and sweep the house and search carefully until she finds it? When she has found it, she calls together her friends and neighbors, saying, 'Rejoice with me, for I have found the coin which I had lost!' In the same way, I tell you, there is joy in the presence of the angels of God over one sinner who repents."*

- Luke 15:22-24 (from the parable of the prodigal son) – *"But the father said to his slaves, 'Quickly bring out the best robe and put it on him, and put a ring on his hand and sandals on his feet; and bring the fattened calf, kill it, and let us eat and celebrate; for this son of mine was dead and has come to life again; he was lost and has been found.' And they began to celebrate."*

  - In these parables, what is the reaction of the coin owner and the father when the coin and the son are found? _____

  _____

  - What might Jesus have been trying to communicate about the heart of God toward us?_____

  _____

  _____

  _____

  _____

5. In our culture, many of us are programmed from childhood to believe that we are supposed to "pull ourselves up by our own bootstraps." But this philosophy runs counter to God's plan for our salvation through Jesus Christ. Read the verses below and underline the phrases that indicate we are helpless to save ourselves:

- Titus 3:3-7 – *"For we also once were foolish ourselves, disobedient, deceived, enslaved to various lusts and pleasures, spending our life in malice and envy, hateful, hating one another. But when the kindness of God our Savior and His love for mankind appeared, He saved us, not on the basis of deeds which we have done in righteousness, but according to His mercy, by the washing of regeneration and renewing by the Holy Spirit, whom He poured out upon us richly through Jesus Christ our Savior, so that being justified by His grace we would be made heirs according to the hope of eternal life."*

- Ephesians 2:8-9 – *"For by grace you have been saved through faith; and that not of yourselves, it is the gift of God; not as a result of works, so that no one may boast."*

- Does it bother you or bless you that you cannot earn or deserve God's salvation? Explain: _____

    _____

    _____

    _____

    _____

    _____

6. Read Matthew 7:24-27 – *"'Therefore everyone who hears these words of Mine and acts on them, may be compared to a wise man who built his house on the rock. And the rain fell, and the floods came, and the winds blew and slammed against that house; and yet it did not fall, for it had been founded on the rock. Everyone who hears these words of Mine and does not act on them, will be like a foolish man who built his house on the sand. The rain fell, and the floods came, and the winds blew*

and slammed against that house; and it fell—and great was its fall.'"

- What kinds of "sand" are people tempted to build their lives upon? Another way to ask this might be: What things do people sometimes trust in to save them, besides Jesus? _____

_____

_____

_____

_____

_____

- How about you? Have you ever looked to anything other than Jesus Christ for salvation or security? Explain: _____

_____

_____

_____

_____

- What are some "storms" that can batter our lives? _____

_____

_____

_____

- What does Jesus say here will happen to houses that are built upon the sand? _____

_____

_____

_____

- Have you learned the lesson of this parable the hard way at any point in your life? Explain: _____

_____

_____

_____

_____

_____

_____

_____

_____

7. The following Scripture passages teach us some things about how a Christian can be used to express God's heart toward people who are not living in close relationship with Him. Fill in the blanks and answer the questions following each verse.

- 2 Corinthians 5:18-20 – *"Now all these things are from God, who reconciled us to Himself through Christ and gave us the ministry of reconciliation, namely, that God was in Christ reconciling the world to Himself, not counting their trespasses against them, and He has committed to us the word of reconciliation. Therefore, we are ambassadors for Christ, as though God were making an appeal through us; we beg you on behalf of Christ, be reconciled to God."*

- God has committed to me the _____
  of _____ and I am Christ's
  _____ in this world.

- What are the typical duties of an ambassador? _____

  _____

  _____

- As an "ambassador for Christ," what is your job? _____

  _____

  _____

  _____

  _____

- Galatians 6:1a – *"Brethren, even if anyone is caught in any trespass, you who are spiritual, restore such a one in a spirit of gentleness ..."*

  - When a brother or sister in Christ has fallen into sin, I am called to _____ him or her in a spirit of _____.

  - Have you ever tried to have a heart-to-heart talk with friends or family members who strayed from God in order to try to help them find their way back to Him? (yes or no)

    _____

  - If you answered "yes" to the question above, what was the most difficult thing about your encounter with the person (or persons)? _____

    _____

_____

_____

_____

- How did they respond? _____

_____

_____

_____

8. What have you learned about salvation from this study? _____

_____

_____

_____

_____

_____

_____

_____

9. Conclude your study by writing out a prayer, thanking God for the times He has "found" and rescued you, praising Him for the unconditional, tender love and grace He lavishes upon you, and asking Him if there is anyone in your life right now to whom you could be Christ's "minister of reconciliation." _____

_____

_____

_____

_____

You're playing golf with a PGA Tour star and he offers to trade scores with you on every hole. Would you do it? Well, God has an even better deal for you—
Let's talk about...

RIGHTEOUSNESS

Only Jesus Gets it All Right

A funny thing happened on my way to learning how to play golf—I figured out that nobody really learns how to play golf. It's a beast that can't be tamed, a foe that can't be conquered, a slippery, slithery reptile of a game that is always one good shot beyond one's grasp.

I remember the first time my husband and I played golf on an actual, nice 18-hole course. I knew that with my knees quickly falling into disrepair, I needed to take up a sport a little more cartilage-friendly than tennis. So while on vacation, we rented some clubs and scheduled a tee time late in the afternoon after most of the real golfers had gone home to soak in their hot tubs.

As we waited in our golf cart near the first tee, the couple ahead of us prepared to tee off. They looked like real golfers. They had all the stuff—furry club covers for their woods, golf shoes, gloves, snazzy golf clothes, the whole package. Being uninformed novices, we didn't know we were supposed to park our carts *behind* the folks teeing off. The approach to the first tee came up from the front, so we parked what we considered a polite distance away, which was about 30 yards in front of and to the side of the tee box.

The man prepared to tee off and we assumed his shot would sail long and straight down the fairway, just like all the big-boy golfers on TV. It never occurred to us that we might be in mortal danger.

We sat there smiling in our little cart as the man launched his golf ball, but in the blink of an eye, his tee shot came crashing into the hood of our cart. We were fine, but that guy's ego was seriously wounded.

It was refreshing to realize that even folks who look like real golfers don't get it right all the time, or even most of the time.

My husband and I have been playing golf sporadically and poorly now for a number of years and we no longer worry about what other golfers think when they spot us trying to blast a ball out of the woods or flailing around in a sand trap. We've figured out that even the best golfers lose balls and miss easy shots.

Turns out that golf is a pretty good metaphor for the Christian life.

When I decided at the age of 19 to sincerely and passionately follow Christ, I felt like a bumbling amateur. In church or at Bible studies, while others seemed to find Scripture passages in Obadiah and Philemon in mere seconds, I was fumbling to locate the table of contents. And when I finally found the passage being discussed, I was awed by the great insights everybody else seemed to get from the Scriptures. I wondered if I'd ever understand God's word like they understood it. My prayers seemed so simple; I didn't know the Christian lingo others so eloquently bantered about.

In short, I felt like everyone around me got it all right, while I was mostly getting it all wrong.

Now that I'm one of those "seasoned veterans" myself, I realize that no one really gets it all right. All of us completely whiff the ball sometimes, or send it 10 yards instead of 200. All of us miss easy "gimme" putts that no one should miss. All of us blast it off the fairway and into the deep woods and occasionally get stuck in life's sandtraps.

But here's the Gospel: Jesus came and played a perfect round, holes-in-one on every hole of life, even the par 5s. And when it's all over, if we've placed our trust in Him, we get to turn in His score-card, not ours.

There are many blessings in obedience and it's the smart thing to do, but there is good news for those times when our tee shots end up in the next county, we launch a pile of balls into the water hazard, or we're stuck in the deep, deep bunkers of life.

When it seems we just can't get it right, we need to remember this simple, profound, grace-filled truth: God doesn't love us because we're good ... He loves us because we're His.

Life is Not a Consumer Test

If you live long enough in this fallen world, you will most likely someday make the unhappy discovery that everything in your freezer/refrigerator is lukewarm. Liquefied goo will ooze from the cracks in the ice cream carton. If you lean in and listen carefully, you will imagine you can hear bacteria reproducing in your ground beef. Your frozen vegetables will go all soft and squishy.

When that happens, you will feel deeply betrayed by this appliance that was supposed to age gracefully and never, ever, ever just quit.

Mine is the voice of experience.

I remember the sad passing of one of our refrigerators. One evening, I noticed a raucous rumble coming from its bowels. My husband turned it off and on and the noise went away, so we naively assumed our cold and frozen things would stay that way overnight. As it turned out, that raucous rumble had, in fact, been a death rattle.

No one really noticed the next morning that the milk was a bit tepid. In fact, nothing seemed amiss until early afternoon when I came home with groceries to put away. As I opened the freezer door, I instantly realized something was very wrong indeed. Our trusty refrigerator had given up the proverbial ghost and taken down some fine food items with it.

Ignoring our bank balance, we had to shop for a new fridge ... pronto. The hunt began the way it always begins at our house when a major purchase is necessary—we opened up our trusty *Consumer Reports Buying Guide* and began learning more than anyone could ever possibly want to know about refrigerators.

Cars, appliances, electronic gizmos, tools, paint—you name it— if we have it at our house, you can bet it had to have earned a good rating in *Consumer Reports*. In fact, if there had been such a thing, I'm convinced that my husband, Joe, would have checked out the 1977 bridal issue of *Consumer Reports* before he married me.

And that makes me pause to give thanks that *Consumer Reports* doesn't rate wives. But if they did …

Cooking skills: Okay, I've come a long way since my newlywed days when beanie-weanies and brownies were my specialties, but my cooking is more utilitarian than gourmet, so I might rank just slightly above average in this category.

Durability: With more than a dozen surgeries in my maintenance records, I don't even want to think about how I might fare in the "durability" category. Let's skip this one, please.

Aesthetic appeal: Comments might include, "has a full set of teeth and a nice twinkle in her eyes, but tends toward gray hair and cellulite."

Yes, indeed, I'm very glad I don't have to rely on consumer research ratings to sell myself to my husband or to anyone else— most especially to God. But there are lots of folks who don't believe that. They think God is like a big *Consumer Reports* tester, tallying up all their assets and defects. At the end of it all, they envision God taking out his clipboard and counting up the scores. Too many black circles and they're on their way to hell; lots of red circles and they get a harp and their own private cloud.

Wrong.

"For by grace you have been saved through faith; and that not of yourselves, it is the gift of God; not as a result of works, so that no one may boast." – Ephesians 2:8-9

God doesn't rate people the way we rate refrigerators. In fact, if God had a "consumer test," only one person could pass it—Jesus, the perfect God-Man. The good news is that as Christians, we get His score beside our names. We get His top rating, even though on our own we run about as well as a refrigerator with a bad compressor.

Theologians call it "imputed righteousness"; I call it a huge, awesome, miraculous RELIEF.

We may be ugly, scratched, dented, and worn out, but in God's eyes, if we're trusting in Christ and not in our own worthiness, we're a "best buy," a real treasure, with value and beauty beyond measure. That's what the amazing grace of God is all about.

Is My Life a Bad Translation?

Somebody call the word police. There's a serial killer on the loose.

The culprit? The people who publish instruction booklets for electronic devices made overseas.

Here are just a few true examples:

From the instructions for a pedometer my mother received: *"Thank you for selecting pedometer. It is an effective to improve your physical strength & fitness. ...Walking is not only a simple exercise method to loose weight but also a favorable solution for inadequate sports. ... The following feathers and instructions would be useful to use this product properly."*

From the instructions for another pedometer: *"This stepping meter can only count correctly under the flat plant. Under the following condition, the stepping meter can't count correctly: moon-walking, wearing sandal, when walking in the tricky condition, vibration without walking."*

From an instruction manual for an Mp3 player I owned: *"Thanks for purchase our digital player. To make you can operate the player expertly as early as possible, we prepare a detailed user manual accessory with the machine ... we edit the manual carefully and we think that the information provided in the manual is right and reliable, while the error and missing is incident, please excuse us ... ."*

And here are some instructions from that same "right and reli-able" booklet: *"Not make strange material into the interior of the production ... not fall the player down during using ... It can be said to be a best works with it's perfect sound quality, rarefied reli-ability and ingenious appearance. We heartily wish it could give you a transcendental enjoyment of digital age."*

That particular Mp3 player sadly didn't give me a "transcen-dental enjoyment of digital age"—it was truly a dud—but I have to say that I did get a bit of transcendental enjoyment from reading the manual. Well, enjoyment mixed with astonishment that these companies didn't hire someone who actually speaks English to write their English instructions. It appears that they simply ran their instruction manuals through a computerized translation program and hoped nobody would notice.

But people notice.

Okay, I think we can learn some things from this. Have you ever been around someone whose Christian walk didn't quite match up to their religious talk? That kind of hollow, self-righteous religion is about as meaningless as one of these bizarro instruction manuals, and a lot less funny.

Jesus got pretty ticked at the way the religious bigwigs of his day "translated" the character and Word of God. Religion had become big business and God's message had been tragically distorted.

It still happens today. Rather than investing time and passion in a real relationship with God, we who call ourselves Christians can too easily settle for simply looking religious, making up rules and spouting clichés to a world that desperately needs to see something genuine, consistent and supernatural.

Acts 4:13 says, *"Now as they observed the confidence of Peter and John and understood that they were uneducated and untrained men, they were amazed, and began to recognize them as having been with Jesus."*

Peter and John were the real deal because they had spent time with Jesus. We'll be real, too, if we pursue a genuine relationship with Him. If we simply "play church" and pat our own self-righteous backs, we come across like a bad translation.

It's not okay to pretend and hope nobody notices.

People notice.

There's a warning in that Mp3 instruction book that says, "not tear, repair or recast it with yourself."

I have no idea what that means in regards to the Mp3 player, but in terms of genuine Christianity, the Bible says it this way: *"I have been crucified with Christ and I no longer live, but Christ lives in me. ..."* (Galatians 2:20).

That's what real righteousness is all about—Jesus living and loving through us—and that's what the world so desperately needs to see.

Let's Talk About Righteousness...Group Discussion Questions

1. Do you feel like you often fail as a Christian and that other believers "get it right" a lot more often and more consistently than you do? Why is comparing ourselves to other Christians unhealthy and even dangerous?

2. Read aloud the following verses: Romans 4:3-5; Philippians 3:3-9; Titus 3:4-6; 1 Corinthians 1:30; and 2 Corinthians 5:21. According to these verses, how is it possible that God sees those who believe in Jesus Christ as righteous?

3. What is the difference between biblical righteousness and self-righteousness?

4. Discuss this statement: "God will never love me any more or any less than He does right now." Do you agree or disagree?

5. If our good deeds don't make us righteous, do our actions even matter? Read James 2:26, Ephesians 2:8-10 and John 15:1-8 and discuss what these verses say about that.

6. How is "playing church" a bad translation of the life Jesus intends for us to live?

7. Fruit trees don't strain to produce fruit—they just grow their roots deep, take in the sun and rain, and good fruit appears. How is this like the righteousness of a true believer in Jesus Christ?

Dig a Little Deeper ... Individual Study

1. Do you feel like you mostly "get it right" or "get it wrong" when it comes to living the Christian life? Explain: _____

   _____

   _____

   _____

   _____

   _____

2. Be honest—do you feel like God loves you because you're His child or because you do "good things"? _____

   _____

   _____

   _____

   _____

   _____

   _____

3. Read Romans 4:3-5: *"For what does the Scripture say? 'Abraham believed God, and it was credited to him as righteousness.' Now to the one who works, his wage is not credited as a favor, but as what is due. But to the one who does not work, but believes in Him who justifies the ungodly, his faith is credited as righteousness."*

   - According to this verse, why was Abraham considered "righteous"? _____

4. Isaiah 64:6 explains what God thinks about people who try to appear righteous by their outward actions but have faithless hearts: *"For all of us have become like one who is unclean, and all our righteous deeds are like a filthy garment; and all of us wither like a leaf, and our iniquities, like the wind, take us away."*

- In this verse, what are people's "righteous acts" compared to?

  _____

- Was the prophet trying to say that we should never do good deeds? Explain: _____

  _____

  _____

  _____

5. Read Philippians 3:3-9 – *"For we are the true circumcision, who worship in the Spirit of God and glory in Christ Jesus and put no confidence in the flesh, although I myself might have confidence even in the flesh. If anyone has a mind to put confidence in the flesh, I far more: circumcised the eighth day, of the nation of Israel, of the tribe of Benjamin, a Hebrew of Hebrews; as to the Law, a Pharisee; as to zeal, a persecutor of the church; as to the righteousness which is in the Law, found blameless. But whatever things were gain to me, those things I have counted as loss for the sake of Christ. More than that, I count all things to be loss in view of the surpassing value of knowing Christ Jesus my Lord, for whom I have suffered the loss of all things,*

and count them but rubbish so that I may gain Christ, and may be found in Him, not having a righteousness of my own derived from the Law, but that which is through faith in Christ, the righteousness which comes from God on the basis of faith ..."

- This verse contrasts two different kinds of righteousness. What are they?

  (1.) Righteousness that comes from the _____

  _____.

  (2.) Righteousness which is through _____ in

  _____.

- Have you always believed that you had to keep certain laws or rules in order to be righteous? Explain: _____

  _____

  _____

  _____

  _____

- If so, what are some of those "laws"? _____

  _____

  _____

  _____

  _____

- Paul lists some of his impressive credentials in this passage. What were some of the things he could have placed his confidence in? _____

  _____

_____

_____

_____

- What does Paul say about the things that could have made him feel righteous in the flesh? _____

_____

_____

_____

- What are some of your strongest attributes and credentials?

_____

_____

_____

_____

- Do those things make you righteous? Why or why not?

_____

_____

_____

_____

- What does make you righteous? _____

_____

6. Read Titus 3:4-6 – "*But when the kindness of God our Savior and His love for mankind appeared, He saved us, not on the basis of deeds which we have done in righteousness, but according to His mercy, by the washing of regeneration and renewing by the*

Holy Spirit, whom He poured out upon us richly through Jesus Christ our Savior..."

- According to this verse, God saves us, not because of _____

  _____

  _____, but because of His _____.

7. Read 1 Corinthians 1:30 – *"But by His doing you are in Christ Jesus, who became to us wisdom from God, and righteousness and sanctification, and redemption..."* and 2 Corinthians 5:21 – *"He made Him who knew no sin to be sin on our behalf, so that we might become the righteousness of God in Him."*

   - Who has become our "righteousness and sanctification, and redemption"? _____

   - Jesus, who had no sin, was made to be _____ for _____, so that we might become the _____ of God.

   - What does this mean to you personally? _____

     _____

     _____

     _____

     _____

     _____

8. If you have placed your trust in Jesus Christ, when God looks at you, He sees the righteousness and holiness of Jesus. How does that make you feel? _____

   _____

_____

_____

_____

_____

9. Read Romans 6:1-2 – *"What shall we say then? Are we to continue in sin so that grace may increase? May it never be! How shall we who died to sin still live in it?"*

   ▪ It might seem like we have "license to sin" because of God's grace, and the righteousness we have in Christ. How does Paul address this wrong assumption in these verses in Romans 6?

   _____

   _____

   _____

   ▪ What do you think it means to be "dead to sin"? _____

   _____

   _____

   _____

10. If you know that through faith in Christ, apart from your works, you are already righteous in the eyes of God, does this motivate you to obey God? Why or why not? _____

   _____

   _____

   _____

   _____

11. Read the verses below and summarize beside each one what it says about doing good works:

- James 2:26 – *"For just as the body without the spirit is dead, so also faith without works is dead."*_____

_____

_____

_____

_____

- Ephesians 2:8-10 – *"For by grace you have been saved through faith; and that not of yourselves, it is the gift of God; not as a result of works, so that no one may boast. For we are His workmanship, created in Christ Jesus for good works, which God prepared beforehand so that we would walk in them."* _____

_____

_____

_____

- From John 15:
  - Verses 1-2 – *"'I am the true vine, and My Father is the vinedresser. Every branch in Me that does not bear fruit, He takes away; and every branch that bears fruit, He prunes it so that it may bear more fruit.'"* _____

_____

_____

_____

- Verses 4-5 – "'*Abide in Me, and I in you. As the branch cannot bear fruit of itself unless it abides in the vine, so neither can you unless you abide in Me. I am the vine, you are the branches; he who abides in Me and I in him, he bears much fruit, for apart from Me you can do nothing.*'"

  _____

  _____

  _____

- Verse 8 – "'*My Father is glorified by this, that you bear much fruit, and so prove to be My disciples.*'" _____

  _____

  _____

  _____

12. Fruit trees don't strain to produce fruit—they just grow their roots deep, take in the sun and rain, and the good fruit appears. How is this like the righteousness of a true follower of Jesus Christ? _____

    _____

    _____

    _____

    _____

    _____

    _____

13. Can you make God love you any more or any less than He does right now? Based on what you've learned in this lesson, why or why not? _____

_____

_____

_____

_____

_____

14. Close with a time of prayer, thanking God for the righteousness He offers through faith in Christ, and for the fact that you don't have to earn His love by being "religious." If you have a sense that you've been trying to earn "brownie points" with God or impress other people by appearing righteous, you can get off that religious treadmill right now. You may use the lines here to write out your prayer if you wish. _____

_____

_____

_____

_____

_____

_____

_____

As any good parent would do, God establishes
borders in the lives of His children.
Sometimes we don't like that, but here's the truth:
All the good stuff is found on God's side of those lines.
Let's talk about ...

BOUNDARIES

On the Wrong Side of the Fence

I used to be concerned that my dog, Winston, might be a wee bit mentally ... uh .... challenged.

Concern has now given way to certainty.

On a recent morning, I went out to call Winston in from his morning romp through the woods. I needed to be on my way to work, but he didn't come when I called—no real surprise, in spite of the doggy obedience diploma hanging on my refrigerator. But I did hear faint, plaintive barking in the distance.

I thought, "Hmmmm, that sure sounds like Winston. I bet he's stuck on the wrong side of the fence again."

Winston has formed a rather annoying habit of running through the woods to the edge of our property and then somehow getting himself stranded on the other side of the fence. We're not sure how he gets over there; obviously, neither is he, because he can never seem to figure out how to get back through.

Maybe it's like one of those *Star Trek* "worm hole" things—a rift in the time-space continuum that opens up just long enough to suck my puppy through. Or maybe Winston's dimmer switch is just set a bit too low, which would be my guess.

My annoyance was reaching a crescendo as I stood on our porch that morning, ready to leave for work, wearing clothes ill-suited for hiking through the woods in search of a wayward dog. Only one of my sons was home at the time and I knew it would be futile to try to pry him from his bed so early on a summer morning, so I went down to our neighbor's house, where some teenagers were spending the week as part of a local missions outreach project. The group had not yet left for their day of ministry, so two boys volunteered to track down Winston for me.

They followed the barking until they found my little beast at the back of our property, across the fence in someone else's yard. But this time, Winston was more thoroughly stuck than usual.

The boys ran back and reported that my dog had gotten himself tangled up in a bunch of twine and had managed to hog-tie himself into total immobility. The boys said Winston didn't seem to really appreciate their first attempts to free him, but they went back to give it another shot.

I prepared to drive my car as close as I could to the scene of Winston's mishap, but just as I got ready to back out of the driveway, one of the boys ran to stop me. He said his buddy had finally been able to free Winston after all. And sure enough, here came my bedraggled pooch, looking like he was wearing a giant twine hairnet over his whole body.

After thanking the guys, I deposited Winston in the house and left for work. On the way, as I stewed over the morning's misadventures, I sensed the Lord interrupting my therapeutic grumbling to impart to me a few take-home lessons:

☐ When God puts up a fence in our lives, it's always better to stay on His side of it. There are such things as right and wrong; light and dark; hope and despair; joy and gloom; peace and turmoil; forgiveness and condemnation; life and death ... and all the good stuff is on God's side of the fence.

❖ If we venture over to the wrong side of the fence, it's fairly easy to get tangled up in some pretty bad stuff. Sin may look harmless, but if we mess around with it, pretty soon we're likely to find ourselves hog-tied and desperate.

❖ If we ever get stuck on the wrong side of life and tangled up in a mess, it's smart to call for God's help. Right away. No need for fancy, eloquent prayers. Just crying out from the heart will do. If my pride ever keeps me from doing that, it's no longer pride—it's plain old stupidity.

God is very real and amazingly practical, and He uses all kinds of down-to-earth things to teach me what He wants me to learn— even a rebellious pup whose life usually serves as a pretty good example of how NOT to live. Thanks, Winston, for all the lessons you learn the hard, hard way, so that if I watch and take heed, maybe I won't have to.

"Can" Doesn't Mean "Should"

When God said, "I will never leave or forsake you," guess what? He meant it. I've discovered that even when I'm on vacation, God isn't. The Holy Spirit never takes a break.

While basking in the warm fall sun at the beach awhile back, I suddenly found myself in God's classroom. The object lesson that day was not one I would have chosen. Ever. It involved a very middle-aged French lady wearing a thong bikini. (And, by the way, I'm not just assuming she was French. I actually heard her speaking French. I'm just sayin'.)

For those of you who are blissfully ignorant of such things, a thong is a string-like swimsuit that more closely resembles dental floss than an article of clothing.

Maybe a wee-tiny percentage of females across the universe could wear a thong without evoking disgust, pity or outrage, but this lady was not a member of that elite group. And even if a woman could wear one, that doesn't mean she should. At least not in public.

And this is the principle God spoke to my heart that day out there on the beach, out there with that French woman parading around in that dental floss: Even if I CAN, it doesn't mean I SHOULD. When it comes to bikinis, I can't, I shouldn't and I won't ... and believe me, I'm doing us all a big, big favor. But there are many other ways to apply this principle, as well. It's not just about thongs.

Just because I have the freedom to say what I want, eat what I want, and push my credit cards to the limit, it doesn't mean I should.

These and other behaviors might be legal, but that sure doesn't make them wise.

The Apostle Paul communicated this principle in 1 Corinthian 6:12: *"All things are lawful for me, but not all things are profitable. All things are lawful for me, but I will not be mastered by anything."*

He also wrote, *"For you were called to freedom, brethren; only do not turn your freedom into an opportunity for the flesh, but through love serve one another."* (Galatians 5:13)

God wants us to be free, but true freedom is found within the wise, loving boundaries He places around our lives. Ask Adam and Eve—God told them they were allowed to eat from ANY tree in the perfect Garden of Eden ... any tree, that is, except one. God knew the fruit from that one tree would open man's eyes to things he would later desperately wish he couldn't see. But God gave Adam and Eve the freedom to choose. They knew they could eat the forbidden fruit, so they did, and their rebellion against God's loving boundary brought death, destruction and bondage.

I'll say it again: Just because we CAN, it doesn't mean we SHOULD.

Are there destructive things you are doing just because you CAN do them? Bad choices, bad habits, bad relationships? Maybe it's time to take inventory, to make sure your choices are bringing life to you and to everyone in your world. Maybe it's time to check your closet and throw out any thong bikinis you find in there.

And hey—I've got an object lesson for you men, too. (Get your mind off the thongs, already!) Friends of ours were missionaries in an Eastern European country where, they said, men were fond of mowing their lawns dressed only in tiny Speedo swimsuits, black socks and dress shoes. Good luck bleaching that mental picture out of your brain. While not particularly edifying, it does serve to further illustrate my point: Just because we CAN, it doesn't mean we SHOULD.

God is Not a Navigating Bully

I just finished taking another trip with Talky Tina and I need to vent my angst.

Talky Tina is the GPS (global positioning system) "broad in a box" who tells my husband how to get where he's going, an exalted position that used to be mine alone. It seems my days as the chief navigating nag are over. Alas, I have been replaced by a bunch of circuits and computer chips.

I'm having a hard time embracing Talky Tina. My husband, on the other hand, has become so dependent on this direction-giving gizmo that I fear the day is approaching when he won't be able to find his way out of our walk-in closet without her.

She has practically become a member of the family.

"Is Talky Tina coming with us today? Did you tell Tina where we're going? Should we bring Tina in so that no one will steal her?"

I've tried to accept her, as you might an irritating pet that was foisted upon you and is now loved by everyone else in the family, but Tina's personality is hard to warm up to. She's so darn bossy. I feel like I'm riding with Hitler.

Talky Tina used to be named Cat Dealy, after the amiable Australian host of the *So You Think You Can Dance* television program. We chose an Australian accent for our GPS system, thinking that would somehow make her incessant yapping less annoying. It didn't.

So, the GPS system formerly known as Cat Dealy is now Talky Tina, aptly named after an especially disturbing character in an old *Twilight Zone* episode we watched while visiting relatives. (After all, nothing says "family time" quite like gathering around to watch *Twilight Zone* together.)

Talky Tina was a doll who was much loved by a sweet little girl who had a very mean stepfather. While in the presence of the girl, Talky Tina only said, "My name is Talky Tina and I love you very much." But when the evil stepfather was alone with the doll, Talky Tina's dark side emerged.

She began threatening the man, her comments growing more sinister over time.

"My name is Talky Tina and I don't think I like you … I think I hate you … I'm going to kill you."

I'll tell you what—it was enough to make you want to pack up your Barbies and haul them to the landfill.

On the way home from that family gathering, our GPS system began relentlessly demanding that we follow her preferred route. My husband and I simultaneously decided, "We need to rename this thing Talky Tina." And so we did.

Tina hasn't actually told us she doesn't like us or threatened to do us in … yet. But when we program a destination into Talky Tina, she becomes VERY agitated if we veer off course. If we try to sneak off the interstate, Tina expresses extreme hostility.

"Recalculate … recalculate … make a u-turn in 50 yards … make a u-turn … MAKE A U-TURN!" she demands.

"We're NOT making a u-turn, Tina! I have to go to the bathroom, so you need to CHILL!" I find myself screaming at this plastic box stuck on our windshield.

Oooh, she does get under my skin. I guess because nobody likes to be nagged and bullied.

I'm thankful that God doesn't try to "steer" us that way. He simply presents straight-up truth and lets us choose whether to follow His loving directions or foolishly go our own way.

But unlike the fallible, irritating Talky Tina, when God whispers, "recalculate," we'd be mighty wise to heed His directions.

Let's Talk About Boundaries … Group Discussion Questions

1. Why and how does God set boundaries in our lives? Do you ever wish He didn't?

2. Why do you think God placed the forbidden fruit in the Garden of Eden? Wouldn't it have been more loving for God to simply not allow any temptation in the Garden?

3. Do you have a hard time believing that "all the good stuff is on God's side of the fence"? Why or why not?

4. When we disobey God and cross boundaries He has established, what are we essentially saying to Him about His goodness and provision?

5. Read this quote from one of the stories and discuss the questions that follow: *"If we venture over to the wrong side of the fence, it's fairly easy to get tangled up in some pretty bad stuff. Sin may look harmless, but if we mess around with it, pretty soon we're likely to find ourselves hog-tied and desperate."*

   ▪ What are some examples in the Bible of people who crossed God's boundaries and found themselves in bad places? (A few hints to get you started: think wandering Jews, belly of a whale, thirty pieces of silver, and dining with the swine.)

   ▪ How about examples from our time or from history? How do the lives of notorious sinners usually end? Discuss some examples.

- How about examples in your own life (rated PG or less, please)? Have you ever wandered off of God's path and gotten yourself into a situation that was painful, uncomfortable, embarrassing, or even devastating?

6. What sometimes keeps us from quickly crying out to God when we find ourselves "over the fence" and into sin?

7. Read 1 Corinthian 6:12 and Galatians 5:13 and discuss the questions that follow:

   - If we are truly free in Christ, can we do anything we want to do? Why or why not?

   - What are some examples of behaviors that we, as Christians, might be free to engage in, but which might not be good for us or those around us?

8. What would you say to someone who feels like God is a bully and His directions and boundaries are annoying (like Talky Tina in the story)?

Dig a Little Deeper ... Individual Study

1. Consider these quotes from one of the stories you just read: *"When God puts up a fence in our lives, it's always better to stay on His side of it"* and *"all the good stuff is found on God's side of the fence."*

   Now read Genesis 2:16-17 – *"The LORD God commanded the man, saying, 'From any tree of the garden you may eat freely;*

from the tree of the knowledge of good and evil you shall not eat, for in the day that you eat from it you will surely die.'"

- God was, in effect, putting up a "fence" or boundary for Adam. What was allowed by God? _____

  _____

  _____

- What was forbidden by God? _____

  _____

- Why do you think God put the forbidden fruit in the garden?

  _____

  _____

  _____

  _____

  _____

- What consequences did God say Adam would experience if he crossed over the line and ate the forbidden fruit? _____

  _____

2. Read Galatians 5:16-23 – *"But I say, walk by the Spirit, and you will not carry out the desire of the flesh. For the flesh sets its desire against the Spirit, and the Spirit against the flesh; for these are in opposition to one another, so that you may not do the things that you please. But if you are led by the Spirit, you are not under the Law. Now the deeds of the flesh are evident, which are: immorality, impurity, sensuality, idolatry, sorcery, enmities, strife, jealousy, outbursts of anger, disputes, dissen-*

sions, factions, envying, drunkenness, carousing, and things like these, of which I forewarn you, just as I have forewarned you, that those who practice such things will not inherit the kingdom of God. But the fruit of the Spirit is love, joy, peace, patience, kindness, goodness, faithfulness, gentleness, self-control; against such things there is no law."

■ According to this passage, what will we experience on "God's side of the fence"? (the "fruit" of the Spirit) _____

_____

_____

_____

■ What will we experience on the "wrong side of the fence," across the boundary God sets for us? (the "deeds of the flesh")

_____

_____

_____

3. Read Jeremiah 17:5-8: *"Thus says the LORD, 'Cursed is the man who trusts in mankind and makes flesh his strength, and whose heart turns away from the LORD. For he will be like a bush in the desert and will not see when prosperity comes, but will live in stony wastes in the wilderness, a land of salt without inhabitant. Blessed is the man who trusts in the LORD and whose trust is the LORD. For he will be like a tree planted by the water, that extends its roots by a stream and will not fear*

when the heat comes; but its leaves will be green, and it will not

be anxious in a year of drought nor cease to yield fruit.'"

- Two sides of a "fence," two ways of living, are contrasted in this passage. They are: trusting in _____ or trusting in _____.

- What difficulties are experienced by those who place their trust in man?_____

  _____

  _____

  _____

- In this passage, what benefits are enjoyed by those who trust in the Lord? _____

  _____

  _____

  _____

4. Have you ever heard it said that when we make something look more appealing than it really is, it's like we're putting lipstick on a pig? That's exactly what Satan does with sin. One of the reasons we end up wandering off God's path and outside of God's boundaries for us is that Satan always does his best to make sin look enticing and desirable. This isn't a new trick; in fact, it's been around since the Garden of Eden.

   - Read Genesis 2:16-17, which records God's actual command to Adam regarding the forbidden fruit: *"The LORD God commanded the man, saying, 'From any tree of the garden you* may eat freely; but from the tree of the knowledge of good and evil you shall not eat, for in the day that you eat from it you will surely die.'"

- Now read Genesis 3:1-6: *"¹Now the serpent was more crafty than any beast of the field which the LORD God had made. And he said to the woman, 'Indeed, has God said, "You shall not eat from any tree of the garden"?' ²The woman said to the serpent, 'From the fruit of the trees of the garden we may eat; ³but from the fruit of the tree which is in the middle of the garden, God has said, "You shall not eat from it or touch it, or you will die."' ⁴The serpent said to the woman, 'You surely will not die! ⁵For God knows that in the day you eat from it your eyes will be opened, and you will be like God, knowing good and evil.' ⁶When the woman saw that the tree was good for food, and that it was a delight to the eyes, and that the tree was desirable to make one wise, she took from its fruit and ate; and she gave also to her husband with her, and he ate."*

- Compare Genesis 2:16-17 to Gen. 3:1. How does Satan misquote and misrepresent God? _____

_____

- Compare Genesis 2:16-17 to Gen. 3:3, where Eve misquotes God, too. What command does Eve add to God's original command to Adam? _____

_____

- By misquoting God's command, did Satan and Eve make God seem unreasonably strict and demanding or more gracious?

  _____

- What does this say to you about the importance of reading, studying and knowing God's word?_____

  _____

  _____

  _____

- In Genesis 3:4-5, what does Satan promise Eve? _____

  _____

  _____

- In Genesis 3:6, Eve allowed her mind to begin thinking about the forbidden fruit. She suddenly believed that the fruit of the tree was good for _____, a _____to the _____ , and also desirable to make one _____.

- After listening to Satan and looking at the forbidden fruit in a different way, what did Eve do next (v. 6)? _____

  _____

  _____

- Why do you think Eve was so focused on the one thing she couldn't have? _____

  _____

  _____

  _____

  _____

- Can you relate to that? Are there things God has said "no" to in your life that you find yourself thinking about, desiring and even pursuing sometimes? Explain: _____

_____

_____

_____

_____

_____

_____

5. Read James 1:13-16 – *"Let no one say when he is tempted, 'I am being tempted by God'; for God cannot be tempted by evil, and He Himself does not tempt anyone. But each one is tempted when he is carried away and enticed by his own lust. Then when lust has conceived, it gives birth to sin; and when sin is accomplished, it brings forth death. Do not be deceived, my beloved brethren."*

- According to this verse, what "drags us away and entices us" to sin? _____

_____

- While we usually equate the word "lust" with sinful, unbridled sexual desire, the broader, biblical definition includes an unhealthy craving or desire for anything. Using that broader definition, what are some things you have lusted for?

_____

_____

_____

_____

- Have you ever been "dragged into sin" by something you wanted? Explain: _____

_____

_____

- When sin is "full-grown," what does it lead to? _____

_____

- We know that everyone who sins does not physically die immediately, so why do you think this verse says, "...*and when sin is accomplished, it brings forth death*"? How are sin and death related? _____

_____

_____

_____

_____

_____

_____

6. Read this quote from the story about Winston the dog: *"If we venture over to the wrong side of the fence, it's fairly easy to get tangled up in some pretty bad stuff. Sin may look harmless, but if we mess around with it, pretty soon we're likely to find ourselves hog-tied and desperate."*

- Now open your Bible and read Genesis 3:7-24. List what Adam and Eve experienced on the "wrong of the fence" in these verses:

  - V. 7: _____
  - V. 8: _____
  - V. 10: _____
  - V. 12: _____
  - V. 16: _____
  - V. 17-18: _____
  - V. 19: _____
  - V. 24: _____

7. Can you think of a time when you gave in to temptation, sinned and then suffered difficult consequences? Explain: _____

   _____

   _____

   _____

   _____

   _____

   _____

8. Consider the Scriptures below and the question that follows:

   - 1 Corinthian 6:12 – *"All things are lawful for me, but not all things are profitable. All things are lawful for me, but I will not be mastered by anything."*

   - Galatians 5:13-14 – *"For you were called to freedom, brethren; only do not turn your freedom into an opportunity for the flesh, but through love serve one another. For the whole Law is fulfilled in one word, in the statement, "YOU SHALL LOVE YOUR NEIGHBOR AS YOURSELF."*

▪ Summarize what you think the Apostle Paul was saying in these verses about our freedom in Christ and the issue of sin:

_____

_____

_____

_____

_____

_____

9. What would you say to someone who feels like God is a bully and His directions and boundaries are annoying (like Talky Tina in the story)? _____

_____

_____

_____

_____

10. What have you learned about God's boundaries from this study?

_____

_____

_____

_____

_____

_____

_____

_____

_____

11. Close by spending some time in prayer. If you know that you are "on the wrong side of the fence" in any area of your life right now, write a prayer below, asking God to rescue you and to bring you back. Don't forget to thank Him for the forgiveness He promises to grant you. _____

_____

_____

_____

_____

_____

_____

_____

_____

_____

_____

_____

_____

_____

_____

_____

_____

_____

*Life in this fallen world can be difficult,
dicey, and dangerous.
That's why we need to know Who is big,
loving and in control.
Let's talk about…*

FEAR

God is Bigger than the Boogey Man

Life can be scary. Watch the news on T.V., read the newspaper, surf the internet, let your mind wander to all the "what ifs,"
and before you know it, fear can wrap its icy fingers around your
heart and squeeze all the peace right out. That's when you need to
remember this simple truth: "God is bigger than the boogey man ..."

It's true, you know—He is. Sarah knows it. She was a three-
year-old who huddled with her mom and two complete strangers
in a hotel bathtub when a freak tornado struck Myrtle Beach, S.C.,
one summer. Sarah and her Mom had been out on a trolley tour
when the first tornado struck. They were able to get off the trolley
and wait out the first storm in an outdoor alcove at a hotel. When it
became apparent that a second twister was coming, Sarah's mom,
Michelle, knocked on the door of a hotel room and asked if she and
her daughter could take refuge there.

The folks who were staying in the room welcomed them in,
so Sarah, Michelle and two strangers all crouched in the bathtub
together, waiting for the furious winds to pass by. Quite understandably, Sarah was scared. Michelle asked her, "What does God want
us to do when we're afraid?" Maybe she expected her little girl to
say, "God wants us to pray," but instead, Sarah burst forth in song.
And what a song it was: *"God is bigger than the boogey man. He's
bigger than Godzilla or the monsters on TV. Oh, God is bigger than
the boogey man and He's watching out for you and me ..."*

The song came from the Veggie Tales video, *Where's God When I'm Scared?* I wonder how many times Michelle and Eric, Sarah's parents, had patiently endured the playing ... and playing ... and playing again ... of that song? I bet there were times when they thought they would pull out their hair if they heard Bob the Tomato and Larry the Cucumber sing one more silly song. We all know how children can be about videos—when you're a kid, there's just no such thing as too much of a good thing. If the horse is fun, you ride him 'til he drops.

"Play it again, play it again," they command.

The Veggie Tale stars were still in seed packets when my guys were little. *The Brave Little Toaster* was the video du jour at the Crum house. It featured a chummy tribe of funny appliances. The lines in the movie were great—the first, second and even third times through, I was chuckling at the one-liners and considering the whole thing an enjoyable experience. By the 16th go-round, I was ready to pull the plug on the whole lot. By the 30th viewing, I was begging to lose consciousness.

But I think that as Michelle and Sarah crouched in that hotel bathtub in Myrtle Beach and Sarah began to sing words of profound, simple truth, all the hours invested in watching Veggie Tales suddenly paid off. The silly song became the voice of God, reminding not just one, but four, of His children that He's big, He sees, He's loving, and He's in control.

What's your boogey man look like today? Like a terrorist? unemployment? cancer? a rebellious child? financial debt?

If you're in the midst of a storm and your heart is huddled up in fear, pause and hear little Sarah sing these words to you:

"You were lying in your bed, you were feeling kind of sleepy,

but you couldn't close your eyes because the room was getting creepy.

Were those eyeballs in the closet? Was that Godzilla down the hall?

There was something big and hairy casting shadows on the wall.

Now your heart is beating like a drum, your skin is getting clammy,

There's a hundred tiny monsters jumping right into your jammies.

What are you going to do? You don't have to do anything, because ...

God is bigger than the boogey man—He's bigger than Godzilla or the monsters on TV

Oh, God is bigger than the boogey man and He's watching out for you and me."

Thanks, for the reminder, Sarah. We need it as never before.

Know Him. Know peace.

My dog's sudden, unexplainable, and exasperating fear of thunder has become one of those things that God is obviously using to teach me lessons I'd rather not learn. Winston's behavior during thunderstorms is so neurotic and inconvenient that it has made me yearn for the cold, relatively calm weather of winter … and hope that my dog doesn't develop a psychotic fear of frost.

Yesterday, I suffered through an entire afternoon, evening and night of stormy weather with PsychoPup. It doesn't even take actual thunder to push Winston's fear button now. He evidently possesses an internal barometer that senses when foul weather is approaching, even if the sun is shining and all seems tranquil. Perhaps I should arrange an audition for him at the Weather Channel.

So keen are my dog's forecasting faculties that he begins to pace and pant before the first visible or audible signs of a storm. I've always heard that when tree leaves turn upside down, a storm is imminent. Now I don't have to check out the trees—as soon as Winston's nerves turn upside down, I know it's time to batten down the hatches.

I wistfully remember when I loved the sound of storms. Such power, such majesty, such a magnificent reminder of the awesomeness of God. But not anymore. Now I'm not reminded of the infinite might of our Creator, but of the insanity of one of His little furry creatures.

As the thunder rumbled yesterday, Winston was a basket case. When it was time to go to bed, he followed us up to our bedroom and I knew we were going to have a problem. Once Winston's paws were planted inside our room, there would be no getting him out without a significant wrestling match.

After all the thunder-induced torment Winston has caused us this summer, I was amazed that I could muster any compassion for him, but I did. I suggested that perhaps we should let him sleep in our room. My husband reluctantly agreed, with an expression on his face that clearly communicated, "I know I'm gonna get to say, 'I told you so' when this is over."

The soothing sounds of rain rhythmically drumming on our roof were interrupted by Winston's panting as he paced around our dark room. Then, we were literally shaken by our dog's futile attempts to burrow under our bed. Finally, just when we thought that he had calmed down and might let us sleep, we heard a bizarre thunking, scratching sound. Upon turning on the light, we discovered that Winston had clumsily climbed into a laundry basket full of clean clothes. A basket case, indeed.

By now, my husband's patience had been pushed past its normally generous limits. Out the bedroom door went Winston. We learned the next day that after his banishment, he sought solace from my son and his girlfriend, who were watching TV downstairs. Unfortunately (and understandably), the young lady didn't appreciate Winston's disturbing habit of parking his hindquarters upon someone's feet when he desires comfort. He's especially fond of bare feet. It's not an altogether pleasant experience, so Winston met with yet more rejection.

So, here's my question to you: Where do you seek refuge when you're afraid? Under the bed? In a laundry basket? Cozied up to someone's feet?

If you chose option number three, you're right, as long as you're cozied up to the right feet. Let's face it—life is full of sudden, thunderous BOOMs! and it can get pretty scary. The possibilities for pain and disaster seem limitless. We can numb our hearts and minds with diversions and denial, but there's only One who can truly calm the storms, our hearts, or both.

Cozy up to the feet of Jesus, tell Him what's scaring you, and entrust your life and loves to Him. As you do, hear His quiet, gentle, supremely confident voice whisper: *"Do not fear, for I am with you; do not anxiously look about you, for I am your God. I will strengthen you, surely I will help you, surely I will uphold you with My righteous right hand."* (Isaiah 41:10)

The old saying is true: No Him, no peace. Know Him, know peace.

It's Good to be in God's Hands

I'm not going to appear very spiritual by admitting this, but having undergone two melanoma surgeries in the past eight weeks, at times I've allowed myself to get altogether too fearful and paranoid about the cancer boogeyman stalking me. I now squint and glare at every little freckle like it's been FedExed to me by the Grim Reaper.

Want to hear something ironic? In the midst of worrying about all of this cancer business, I almost ended up as road kill at the grocery store. I nearly got taken out of this world, not by cancer, but by a woman driving through a parking lot.

The week before Christmas, my husband and I were taking groceries to our car and I somehow didn't notice a ginormous SUV barreling toward me. Behind the wheel was a woman in a hurry who was not caring about speed limits or pedestrian right-of-way issues at that moment.

When an oblivious pedestrian (me) meets up with an oblivious driver (her), the driver always wins, so I surely would've been mowed down had my hubby not yelled "STOPPPPPPPP!" in the nick of time.

I didn't need another adrenaline blast—after all, I was still shell-shocked from paying nearly 70 bucks for our Christmas roast—but I got quite a jolt when I realized that my roast and I had come within a half-step of being catapulted into eternity.

I learned two things from this experience: 1.) Never interfere with a woman on a shopping mission—the driver of that car had a steely look in her eye that screamed, "I dare you to get between me and my Christmas ham"; and 2.) Unhealthy fear is a huge waste of time because something we haven't even bothered to be afraid of may well be the thing that gets us.

Let's face it, we really never know for sure what's going to go down in the course of a day. I should do what I reasonably can to take care of myself, but ultimately, my life is in God's hands. The desire to control and the inclination to doubt come so naturally; trusting God is a challenge.

It's easy for me to pontificate about having faith in God; it's a heck of a lot harder to trust Him and His promises when life gets unexpectedly dicey.

Do I *truly* believe what I say I believe? Is my faith in God real enough to keep my heart peaceful when living each day feels a bit like tip-toeing through a minefield?

I've wrestled aplenty in recent months, but at the end of each day, by the grace of God, I've held on to Him and what He says. We're all trusting someone or something; no one else has a rèsumè like God's.

This world can be a scary place, indeed. Scary, but not spinning out of control. I'm convinced a good God is at the helm, and perhaps the highest form of worship and expression of faith I can offer is to simply relax in His care, come what may.

A character in C.S. Lewis' book, *The Lion, the Witch and the Wardrobe*, makes an interesting observation about Aslan, the mighty lion who allegorically represents God in the story. When asked if Aslan is safe, the character replies: "Who said anything about safe? 'Course he isn't safe. But he's good. He's the King, I tell you."

And I tell you, I'm clinging to the fire-tested assurance that a good God, the King above all kings, holds me in His strong, loving hands. I'm quite sure there's no better place to be and it's where I plan to stay.

"Fear not," God says.

Sounds like a good plan to me.

Let's Talk About Fear ... Group Discussion Questions

1. What are people most afraid of these days?

2. What do you usually do when you are afraid?

3. Are there healthy fears and unhealthy fears? Give examples of each.

4. The Scriptures often say, "I will not fear" and command us, "Do not be afraid." This implies we have a choice in the matter. Do you feel like you have a choice to fear or not to fear?

5. What do you think our unhealthy fears communicate to God and about God?

6. Read Psalm 46:1-3. Have you ever started to feel fearful and then successfully moved from fear to faith by turning your thoughts toward God?

7. The Bible talks about God being a "strong tower," a "hiding place" or a "refuge." What does this mean in practical terms to you?

8. Discuss the idea that while God is good, He is not necessarily "safe." In what sense is God unsafe? In what sense is He safe?

9. Read 1 John 4:16-18. Verse 18 in the King James translation includes this phrase: "fear hath torment." In what ways is fear tormenting?

10. While we're told over and over not to fear, we are also commanded to have a healthy fear of God. What does this mean? What does it not mean?

11. Close this session with a prayer time, allowing group members to ask God to replace any unhealthy fears with faith in His sovereignty and love.

Dig a Little Deeper ... Individual Study

1. What are some of the "boogeymen" in your life—things you are afraid of? _____

   _____

   _____

2. Read Psalm 46:1-3 –*"God is our refuge and strength, a very present help in trouble. Therefore we will not fear, though the earth should change and though the mountains slip into the heart of the sea; though its waters roar and foam, though the mountains quake at its swelling pride."*

   - God says He is our refuge, strength and help in trouble, but the world offers a whole array of substitutes—other things we can turn to when we're afraid. Name some of these substitutes: _____

     _____

     _____

   - When you have been in trouble, have you ever turned to one of the world's substitutes? _____ Did you find it to be truly helpful? _____Why or why not?_____

     _____

     _____

3. Read 1 John 4:16-18 -- *"We have come to know and have believed the love which God has for us. God is love, and the one who abides in love abides in God, and God abides in him. By this, love is perfected with us, so that we may have confidence in the day of judgment; because as He is, so also are we in this world. There is no fear in love; but perfect love casts out fear, because fear involves punishment, and the one who fears is not perfected in love."*

- Does knowing how much God loves you help you deal with fear? Why or why not? _____

  _____

  _____

  _____

  _____

- A phrase in the 1 John passage above, as translated in the *New American Standard* version of the Bible says, "fear involves punishment" (v. 18); in the *King James* version it reads this way: "fear hath torment." In what ways is fear tormenting?

  _____

  _____

  _____

  _____

  _____

4. It is scary to feel like other people control your destiny—that you are at the mercy of imperfect, selfish and sometimes cruel

people. Read the verses below and answer this question in the blank beside each verse: *What reason(s) are you given in this verse not to fear people?*

- Psalm 56:4 – *"In God, whose word I praise, in God I have put my trust; I shall not be afraid. What can mere man do to me?"* _____

_____

_____

- Psalm 118:6 – *"The LORD is for me; I will not fear; what can man do to me?"* _____

_____

_____

- Psalm 27:1 – *"The LORD is my light and my salvation; whom shall I fear? The LORD is the defense of my life; whom shall I dread?"* _____

_____

_____

- Isaiah 49:15-16 – *"Can a woman forget her nursing child and have no compassion on the son of her womb? Even these may forget, but I will not forget you. Behold, I have inscribed you on the palms of My hands; your walls are continually before Me."* _____

_____

_____

- Matthew 10:28 – *"Do not fear those who kill the body but are unable to kill the soul; but rather fear Him who is able to destroy both soul and body in hell."* _____

_____

_____

_____

5. Read the verses below and answer the following question after each: *According to this verse, what can we do to combat fear in our lives?*

- Psalm 34:4-5 – *"I sought the LORD, and He answered me; He delivered me from all my fears. Those who look to Him are radiant; their faces are never covered with shame."*

_____

_____

_____

_____

- Isaiah 26:3 – *"Thou wilt keep him in perfect peace whose mind is stayed on Thee; because he trusteth in Thee."* (*King James Version*) _____

_____

_____

6. Read the verses below and answer the questions that follow.

- Psalm 34:8 – *"O taste and see that the LORD is good; how blessed is the man who takes refuge in Him!"*

- Psalm 118:8-9 – *"It is better to take refuge in the LORD than to trust in man. It is better to take refuge in the LORD than to trust in princes."*

- Psalm 94:22 – *"But the LORD has been my stronghold, and my God the rock of my refuge."*

- Proverbs 18:10 – *"The name of the LORD is a strong tower; the righteous runs into it and is safe."*

- What comes to your mind when you hear the words "refuge," "fortress" and "tower"? _____

  _____

- What do you think it means, practically speaking, to make the Lord your refuge, fortress and strong tower? _____

  _____

  _____

  _____

7. The Bible talks about one fear that is a good fear—a healthy fear of God. Read all the verses below and answer the questions that follow.

   - Exodus 20:20 – *"Moses said to the people, 'Do not be afraid; for God has come in order to test you, and in order that the fear of Him may remain with you, so that you may not sin.'"*

   - Proverbs 1:7 – *"The fear of the LORD is the beginning of knowledge; fools despise wisdom and instruction."*

   - Proverbs 31:30 – *"Charm is deceitful and beauty is vain, but a woman who fears the LORD, she shall be praised."*

- Luke 12:4-5 – *"'I say to you, My friends, do not be afraid of those who kill the body and after that have no more that they can do. But I will warn you whom to fear: fear the One who, after He has killed, has authority to cast into hell; yes, I tell you, fear Him!'"*

- 1 Peter 1:17 – *"If you address as Father the One who impartially judges according to each one's work, conduct yourselves in fear during the time of your stay on earth ..."*

- When we are told to "fear God," the literal meaning is to have reverence or awe. How would you describe in your own words what it means to have a healthy fear of God? _____

_____

_____

_____

- Scriptures like Exodus 20:20 tell us not to be afraid, but they also indicate that fearing God is a good thing. Explain why that isn't a contradiction: _____

_____

_____

_____

_____

_____

- Did you grow up having no fear of God at all (didn't really think about God), a healthy fear of God (biblical rever-

ence and awe), or an unhealthy fear of God (terror, dread)?
Explain: _____

_____

_____

_____

- What about now? Do you have no fear, a healthy fear or an unhealthy fear of God? Explain: _____

_____

_____

_____

8. It's been said that an unhealthy fear of anything is actually a distorted form of faith—that to be afraid of someone or something is to have faith in the power of that person or thing over us. While we are instructed to have a healthy fear of God, the Bible tells us that God *"has not given us a spirit of fear..."* (1 Timothy 1:7) and commands us repeatedly not to be afraid. Think about the things you are afraid of and consider this: "Is this fear evidence that I am putting my faith in a power other than God's power?" What do you think?_____

_____

_____

_____

_____

_____

_____

9. What message does it send to God when we allow fear to keep us from doing something He wants us to do?_____

_____

_____

_____

_____

10. Is there anything you would do (that you are not currently doing) if you weren't afraid of failing or getting hurt? _____

_____

_____

_____

_____

11. What have you learned about fear from this study?_____

_____

_____

_____

_____

_____

12. End this study with a prayer time, expressing to God all the things you are afraid of and asking Him to replace each unhealthy fear with faith in His sovereignty and love. You may write out your prayer on the lines below if you wish...

_____

_____

It's easy to snicker at the Israelites of Isaiah's day who took a block of wood, carved out an idol, and then fell down and worshipped it.
But are we really so different?
Let's talk about…

IDOLATRY

A Paper Daddy is a Poor Substitute

When my sons were very young and understandably high-main-tenance, I dreaded those times when my husband had to go out of town on business trips. Many single parents do an amazing job, but when Joe was gone and I was temporarily forced to be both mom and dad to my sons, my feet just didn't feel big enough to fill both pairs of shoes.

We always managed to survive, but it wasn't always easy and it was never fun. It certainly didn't help that my sons always seemed to come down with stomach bugs when Joe was gone. I don't do stomach bugs well. Fragile gag reflex, you know. Verrrrrrry fragile. Joe was much better at handling such things, and I never hesitated to praise him for his iron constitution.

But one time when Joe was out of town, the son on the top bunk bed came down with an especially nasty virus in the middle of the night. Think "Niagra Falls." I begged for Jesus to come back at that moment. He didn't.

My daughter-in-law Jessi told me that when she was a little girl and her father had to be away on a three-week business trip, she made a nearly life-size, paper cut-out of a man and christened him Paper Daddy. Jessi said Paper Daddy sat at the table with them during meals (they even fixed him a plate of food), watched T.V. with them, and generally became an esteemed member of the family.

Of course, Paper Daddy was a poor substitute for the real thing. He couldn't hug, snuggle, read stories, or give piggyback rides. He was cold, fragile and lifeless.

And so it is with the "paper gods" we make when we don't have a real relationship with the one true God.

Sometimes our paper god looks a bit like Santa Claus—a jolly old soul who in the end, we imagine, will smile and welcome every-body into Heaven, saying, "Oh, shucks, come on in—I didn't really mean all that stuff about hell." This cardboard deity doesn't bear any resemblance to the God of the Bible, but he makes us feel good, and we sure do like to feel good.

Sometimes our paper god looks just like us because we like to play god. We're not good at it, but we like it. We like to exalt and rely upon our own abilities and resources. We imagine that pleasing ourselves is our highest calling.

Paper gods can look like anything—bank accounts, prestigious positions, material possessions, fame, other people. It's easy to get out the paper and scissors and whip up something to worship.

But what happens when the medical tests come back and the diagnosis is cancer? Or when we find out our teenager is addicted to drugs? Or when our mother is stricken with Alzheimer's? Or when the business fails or the marriage becomes a nightmare?

The prophet Isaiah understood. He was God's spokesman to the worshippers of false deities in his day, saying, *"When you cry out for help, let your collection of idols save you! The wind will carry all of them off, a mere breath will blow them away. But the man who makes Me his refuge will inherit the land and possess My holy mountain.”* (Isaiah 57:13)

Paper gods may make us feel deceptively religious and secure when life is going well, but when things go awry, an imaginary "higher power" is woefully inadequate. When the winds rage, I want to know my God can still them, or help me stand through the tempest. When my heart is broken, I need the God who calls Himself "the God of all hope," the Wonderful Counselor and Comforter.

The true God may not always act exactly when and how we want Him to act, but He's God ... and we're not ... and neither is anything or anyone else. He knows us intimately, loves us passionately, and He never, ever fails or changes.

When I need a refuge, I don't want one made of paper. Paper wilts in a storm. I want a rock, and that rock is Jesus.

"For who is God besides the Lord? And who is the Rock except our God?" – Psalm 18:31

"But the LORD has become my fortress, and my God the rock in whom I take refuge." – Psalm 94:22

Are You a Gutterpecker?

"Okay, who in the world is up on my roof with a jackhammer? Or, wait … what IS that? Is somebody spraying my house with a machine gun?"

That's what I wondered recently when my afternoon nap was interrupted by a loud, fast and persistent rat-a-tat noise coming from my roof.

Rat-a-tat, rat-a-tat, rat-a-tat, pause. Rat-a-tat, rat-a-tat, rat-a-tat, pause.

After about the fourth stanza, I went outside to investigate. As I opened the front door, the ruckus stopped, but when I parked myself back on the couch, the rat-a-tatting started up again. Over and over this routine was repeated. I felt like I was stuck in a cartoon.

The commotion cranked up again the next day, but this time I was stealthy enough to spot a woodpecker fleeing the scene. Ah-ha! That rascal was pecking on our gutters.

A low-down gutterpecker.

We live in the middle of a bunch of trees packed with all the succulent stuff God intended for woodpeckers to eat. What kind of self-respecting bird would turn up his beak at those and choose instead to peck on aluminum gutters?

My new nemesis does occasionally dine at our birdfeeders and we're always glad to see him at our birdie buffet. He's really quite pretty with his red head and black stripes. But why did he decide our gutters are part of the smorgasbord?

I suspect that perhaps he has a case of woodpecker pica.

Pica is an actual human disease which is defined as "the persistent eating of nonnutritive substances for at least one month." We're not talking Big Macs and Twinkies here. If one can believe what one reads on the internet (yeah, right), then individuals diagnosed with pica have been reported to consume such things as clay, dirt, sand, stones, pebbles, hair, feces, lead, laundry starch, vinyl gloves, plastic, pencil erasers, fingernails, paper, paint chips, coal, chalk, wood, plaster, light bulbs, needles, string, cigarette butts and ashes, wire, burnt matches, wax, paint, buttons, and soap.

Yuck.

Some forms of pica are common enough to warrant their own medical names. Here are a few: *xylophagia*—eating wooden toothpicks; *coniophagia*—eating dust; *geophagia*—eating clay or dirt; *amylophagia*—eating laundry starch and paste; *trichophagia*—eating hair.

Let me say it again: Yuck.

I read that in 1985, a man had 212 objects removed from his stomach, including 53 toothbrushes, two razors, two telescopic antennas, and 150 handles of disposable razors.

Pretty crazy, huh? Crazy, but allegedly true. People actually have pica, and so does at least one woodpecker who has acquired a taste for aluminum. Okay, so maybe most of us can't relate to this physical affliction, but I'm guessing that probably all of us have a touch of spiritual and emotional pica.

We're all trying to scratch up enough love, acceptance, fulfillment, security and peace to get us through this life, and sometimes we look in the wrong places to find something—anything—to fill our hungry hearts.

We go pecking around in the gutters of this world when God is shouting for us to come to Him and discover what it means to be truly fed and satisfied. All the good stuff is found in Jesus. No use looking in the gutters when there's a feeder full of satisfaction right around the corner, just a prayer away.

"The eyes of all look to You, and You give them their food in due time … .The LORD is near to all who call upon Him, to all who call upon Him in truth. He will fulfill the desire of those who fear Him; He will also hear their cry and will save them."– Psalm 145:15, 18-19

Divine Bovines and Heavenly Eggs?

Have you noticed all the news stories about people seeing what they interpret as "holy" images etched, hatched, birthed and baked on all kinds of weird things?

One lady, for example, was dead sure she could see the face of Jesus on her iron. This snagged her a two-minute gig on the T.V. news. The woman said she was going through a hard time and the image on her iron pulled her through. Okay, then.

Another lady appeared on the news with a pancake that has, she said, the face of the Virgin Mary on it. This woman is keeping her heavenly flapjack in the freezer so she can pull it out and be encouraged anytime she needs a lift.

Then there's the farmer whose hen laid an egg that has a crinkly cross on the end of it. I'm guessing that egg is not destined to become an omelet. In fact, the farmer said he is thinking about selling it on Ebay to someone who finds that sort of thing inspiring. It won't be me.

A dairy farmer in Connecticut had a Holstein heifer that birthed a calf, dubbed the "holy cow" or "divine bovine," with a white marking on its head "in the approximate shape of a cross." According to a newspaper article, "the farmer said he thinks the marking may be a message from above, though he's still trying to figure out what that message might be."

Um ... I'm thinking that if God really wants to communicate a "message from above," we won't be left wondering what that message is. And He probably won't have to communicate it through an iron or a pancake or an egg or a cow, holy or not.

As a matter of fact, here's something newsworthy—God HAS already spoken to us, in His word and through His son, Jesus.

As it says in Hebrews 1:1-2: *"God ... in these last days has spoken to us in His son, whom He appointed heir of all things, through whom also He made the world."*

That passage in Hebrews goes on to say that Jesus is the *"exact representation of His (God's) nature."* So, hello, if we're looking to hear from God, there He is—right there in Jesus, right there on the pages of the Bible. His character is described, His personality is revealed, His power is demonstrated, and His desires are expressed.

My oldest son came over awhile back to make some toast and to borrow our fancy digital camera. When the toast was ready, Ryan laid it on the kitchen table and started taking pictures of it. That's a bit weird, I thought, even though weird is more often the rule than the exception around our house.

Turns out Ryan needed a high-quality picture of a piece of toast for a software application he was writing for iPhones. The application would let a person superimpose an image of his or her face over the toast picture. Like me, Ryan was poking a bit of fun at all this hoopla over people seeing heavenly images on mundane objects.

No doubt God loves to reveal Himself to those who honestly seek Him. He wants to be found by us and He can show up anyway, anytime, anywhere He wants to.

But we'd be wise to look to the Bible for His encouragement, instruction and inspiration, for it's a sure thing—we'll always find Him there.

Let's Talk About Idolatry ... Group Discussion Questions

1. How would you define an idol? How can we know if we've made something or someone an idol?

2. What are some of the most obvious idols for many people in our country? Is there any such thing as a harmless idol? Why or why not?

3. Variations of the following quote have been attributed to both 18th-century philosopher Jean-Jacques Rousseau and Mark Twain: "In the beginning, God created man in His own image; ever since, man has returned the compliment."

   ▪ What evidence do you find in our culture that people frequently try to turn God into a "paper god"—to pretend that He is whatever they want Him to be?

   ▪ In what ways are even committed Christians tempted to fashion God to suit their preferences and desires?

4. Discuss this statement: If God were small enough for us to understand, He would be too small to worship.

   ▪ Do you find it scary or comforting that there are things about God that we can't completely understand?

5. Why do you think God chose to make "You shall have no other gods before me" the very first of the Ten Commandments?

6. Read Jeremiah 17:5-8 and discuss the descriptions given in this passage of two kinds of people: those who trust in human strength and those who trust in the Lord.

7. Why do you think some people put so much stock in seeing allegedly "heavenly images" on objects like irons or pancakes? Do you think this is valid or bogus? Dangerous or harmless?

Dig a Little Deeper ... Individual Study

1. How would you define an idol? _____

_____

_____

_____

2. The dictionary defines an idol as "a representation or symbol of an object of worship; a false god; a likeness of something; a form or appearance visible but without substance; an object of extreme devotion; a false conception." In the story you read about the "Paper Daddy," some of the idols (or "paper gods") mentioned include the following: a Santa-like god who gives us whatever we want, our bank accounts, powerful positions, material possessions, other people, and even ourselves.

   ▪ Have any of these or other things ever become idols to you? Explain: _____

_____

_____

_____

_____

- Beside each potential "idol" listed below, there is a Scripture reference. Read each verse and write any insights you may gain about these common false gods:

- **Money:** Luke 18:18-23 – *"A ruler questioned Him, saying, 'Good Teacher, what shall I do to inherit eternal life?' And Jesus said to him, 'Why do you call Me good? No one is good except God alone. You know the commandments, 'DO NOT COMMIT ADULTERY, DO NOT MURDER, DO NOT STEAL, DO NOT BEAR FALSE WITNESS, HONOR YOUR FATHER AND MOTHER.' And he said, 'All these things I have kept from my youth.' When Jesus heard this, He said to him, 'One thing you still lack; sell all that you possess and distribute it to the poor, and you shall have treasure in heaven; and come, follow Me.' But when he had heard these things, he became very sad, for he was extremely rich.*

- What does this passage say to you about idolizing money?

  _____

  _____

  _____

- **Material possessions:** Luke 12:16-21 – *"And He told them a parable, saying, 'The land of a rich man was very productive. And he began reasoning to himself, saying, "What shall I do, since I have no place to store my crops?" Then he said, "This is what I will do: I will tear down my barns and build larger ones, and there I will store all my grain and my goods.*

And I will say to my soul, 'Soul, you have many goods laid up for many years to come; take your ease, eat, drink and be merry.'" But God said to him, "You fool! This very night your soul is required of you; and now who will own what you have prepared?"' So is the man who stores up treasure for himself, and is not rich toward God."

- What does this passage say to you about idolizing possessions? _____

  _____

- **Relationships:** Matthew 10:37 – (Jesus speaking): *"He who loves father or mother more than Me is not worthy of Me; and he who loves son or daughter more than Me is not worthy of Me."*

- What does this passage say to you about idolizing people?

  _____

  _____

- **Self:** Matthew 16:24-25 – *"Then Jesus said to His disciples, 'If anyone wishes to come after Me, he must deny himself, and take up his cross and follow Me. For whoever wishes to save his life will lose it; but whoever loses his life for My sake will find it.'"*

- What does this passage say to you about idolizing yourself?

  _____

  _____

  _____

3. The prophet Isaiah tried to make people understand how crazy it is to worship idols. Read Isaiah 44:16-19 (he is referring here to idols carved out of wood) – *"Half of it he burns in the fire; over this half he eats meat as he roasts a roast and is satisfied. He also warms himself and says, 'Aha! I am warm, I have seen the fire.' But the rest of it he makes into a god, his graven image. He falls down before it and worships; he also prays to it and says, 'Deliver me, for you are my god.' They do not know, nor do they understand, for He has smeared over their eyes so that they cannot see and their hearts so that they cannot comprehend. No one recalls, nor is there knowledge or understanding to say, 'I have burned half of it in the fire, and also have baked bread over its coals. I roast meat and eat it. Then I make the rest of it into an abomination, I fall down before a block of wood!'"*

- How would you summarize what Isaiah was saying here?

  _____

  _____

  _____

  _____

- Consider this statement: *If God were small enough for us to understand, He would be too small to worship.* How does this relate to the passage from Isaiah you just read? _____

  _____

  _____

  _____

_____

_____

_____

4. In Exodus 20, we find what we commonly refer to as the Ten Commandments. Read Exodus 20:1-6 – *"Then God spoke all these words, saying, 'I am the LORD your God, who brought you out of the land of Egypt, out of the house of slavery. You shall have no other gods before Me. You shall not make for yourself an idol, or any likeness of what is in heaven above or on the earth beneath or in the water under the earth. You shall not worship them or serve them; for I, the LORD your God, am a jealous God, visiting the iniquity of the fathers on the children, on the third and the fourth generations of those who hate Me, but showing lovingkindness to thousands, to those who love Me and keep My commandments.'"*

  ▪ Why do you think that God chose to make "You shall have no other gods before me" the very first commandment in this section of Scripture? _____

  _____

  _____

  _____

  _____

5. Exodus 32 recounts the grievous sin committed by the children of Israel when they formed and worshipped a golden calf while

Moses was up on a mountain meeting with God. Read Exodus 32 and answer the following questions:

- In verse 1, we get a clue about the emotion that may have prompted the Israelites to ask Aaron to make an idol for them. What were the Israelites worried about? _____

_____

- Do you see a connection in your own life between feeling fearful, worried or anxious and being tempted to turn to a false god? Explain: _____

_____

_____

- When we turn to other "gods" because we think they will meet our needs, what are we really saying to the one, true God? _____

_____

_____

- In verse 4, the Israelites declared that the golden calf Aaron made for them was the "god" who brought them up from the land of Egypt. Now read Leviticus 11:45 and Exodus 32:10. Can you understand why God's anger burned against the Israelites? Explain: _____

_____

_____

_____

6. There are several different Hebrew words found in the Old Testament that are translated "idol" in the English language. Some of those words are listed below, along with their literal definitions. Beside each, explain why this is an accurate definition for a false god:

- Aven – nothingness : _____
- Bosheth – shameful thing: _____
- Billulim – dung, refuse: _____
- Tselem – shadow: _____
- Atsab – something fashioned or labored over: _____

7. Read Isaiah 42:17 – *"They will be turned back and be utterly put to shame, who trust in idols, who say to molten images, 'You are our gods.'"*

- According to this verse, what will happen to people who trust in idols? _____

  _____

8. Read Isaiah 57:13a – *"When you cry out, let your collection of idols deliver you. But the wind will carry all of them up, and a breath will take them away."*

- According to this verse, what will happen to idols? _____

  _____

9. Read Jeremiah 17:5-8 – *"Thus says the LORD, 'Cursed is the man who trusts in mankind and makes flesh his strength, and whose heart turns away from the LORD. For he will be like a bush in the desert and will not see when prosperity comes,*

but will live in stony wastes in the wilderness, a land of salt without inhabitant. Blessed is the man who trusts in the LORD and whose trust is the LORD. For he will be like a tree planted by the water, that extends its roots by a stream and will not fear when the heat comes; but its leaves will be green, and it will not be anxious in a year of drought nor cease to yield fruit.'"

- Below, write phrases found in this passage that describe a person who puts his trust in people and whose heart turns away from the Lord: _____

_____

_____

_____

_____

- To what does this passage compare a person who trusts God?
  A _____ planted by the _____.

- There are four benefits listed here for the person who chooses to trust God, not idols. Fill in the blanks below and then explain in your own words what you think these benefits mean to you personally:

  1. He will not _____ when the _____ comes. What this means to you: _____

  _____

  _____

2. His _____ will be _____. What this
   means to you: _____

   _____

   _____

   _____

3. He will not be _____ in a year of _____.
   What this means to you: _____

   _____

   _____

   _____

4. He will not cease to _____. What this means
   to you: _____

   _____

   _____

   _____

10. Read the following verses and answer the question that follows:
    - Psalm 18:31 – *"For who is God, but the LORD? And who is a rock, except our God ...?"*
    - Psalm 94:22 – *"But the LORD has been my stronghold, and my God the rock of my refuge."*
    - Isaiah 26:4 – *"Trust in the LORD forever, for in GOD the LORD, we have an everlasting Rock."*
    - In what ways is the one, true God like a rock? _____

      _____

      _____

11. Read 2 Chronicles 16:9a – "*For the eyes of the LORD move to and fro throughout the earth that He may strongly support those whose heart is completely His.*"

    ▪ What is God looking for? _____

    ▪ What does God promise to those whose hearts are fully committed to Him? _____

    _____

12. What have you learned about idolatry from this study?

    _____

    _____

    _____

    _____

    _____

    _____

    _____

    _____

13. Close this study with a time of prayer. If you realize you have idols in your life—things or people you have made more important than God—confess that to God, receive His forgiveness, and reaffirm that Jesus is the only Lord of your life. You may use the lines below to write out your prayer, if you wish.

    _____

    _____

    _____

    _____

Listen. Encourage. Exhort. Edify.
How hard can it be?
Real hard, apparently.
Let's talk about …

COMMUNICATION

The Lost Art of Sweet Talk

"Like apples of gold in settings of silver is a word spoken in right circumstances," said wise King Solomon in Proverbs. With hundreds of wives, I bet Solomon learned the hard way that the opposite is also true—the wrong thing said at the wrong time can make you wish you'd had your lips sewn shut.

For better or worse, our tongues can pack a punch. A bomb or a balm, a weapon of mass destruction or an instrument of healing— which will it be?

With that in mind, let me suggest to husbands everywhere some things NOT to say to your wives, gleaned from my own experiences and those of friends. Pay attention, please ...

When I was great with child (truly a euphemism of biblical proportions), I felt like a balloon being slowly inflated to fly in the Macy's Thanksgiving Day Parade. That's why when my husband began calling me the "S.S. Crum" and making foghorn noises as I lumbered by, it didn't exactly feel like I was being blessed with "apples of gold."

A friend's husband told her it looked like God took two blobs of Play-Doh and rolled them vigorously between His hands when He created her legs.

Another friend was trying to have a serious conversation with her husband while he was watching a T.V. interview with a football coach. As she poured out her heart, she noticed that her beloved's eyes were glazed over and locked in on the coach. She then realized that her hubby was mindlessly chanting, "Uh huh ... uh huh" while steadily turning up the volume on the T.V. to drown her out. Bet you won't find that move in the "Handbook for Blissful Marriages."

One fellow I know, in a misguided effort to be encouraging, told his wife that her fat didn't jiggle around nearly as much as she imagined it did. "Your fat must be so tightly compacted in there, it can't jiggle," he said. Methinks that verbal love arrow missed its mark.

I don't know who 10-year-old Ricky is, but I got an email quoting Ricky's sage advice to men: "Tell your wife she looks pretty even if she looks like a truck." Maybe Ricky should travel the country conducting "Be Suave" seminars for conversationally retarded males. Or not.

Men, you might want to check out the Song of Solomon in the Bible for some tips on sweet-talking your honey: *"Your hair is like a flock of goats that have descended from Mount Gilead. Your teeth are like a flock of newly shorn ewes which have come up from their washing...your temples are like a slice of pomegranate ... your neck is like the tower of David built with rows of stones, on which are hung a thousand shields ... your breasts are like two fawns, twins of a gazelle, which feed among the lilies."*

Okay, so you might want to update those goat, sheep and gazelle analogies, and I'm not real sure about the pomegranate thing, but I think Solomon was on the right track.

Or if your neck is just a bit red, perhaps you could borrow a few lines from this quaint poem that was passed on to me:

"Yo're as satisfy'n as okry jist a fryin' in the pan;

yo're as fragrant as snuff right out of the can. ...

On special occasions, when you shave under yore arms,

well I'm in hawg heaven, and awed by your charms. ...

Me'n you's like a Moon Pie with a RC cold drank,

we go together like a skunk goes with stank."

Guys, please don't tell us that our legs look like strands of rolled Play-Doh, that we move like a cruise ship, or that our fat is packed so tightly that it can't jiggle. You also might want to avoid any references to skunks, and never, ever, ever turn up the TV volume while we're talking to you.

And one last tip: Try to stifle comments like the one I received the other night from my beloved when he was trying to encourage me about some recent weight loss and sported out with, "Hey, I didn't know you had ribs."

Much better and safer to keep it sincere and simple, like God does:

"For the mountains may be removed and the hills may shake, but My lovingkindness will not be removed from you." (Isaiah 54:10).

"I have loved you with an everlasting love." (Jeremiah 31:3)

"Do not fear, for I have redeemed you; I have called you by name; you are Mine! When you pass through the waters, I will be with you..."(Isaiah 43:1-2).

"For God so loved the world that He gave His only begotten Son..."(John 3:16).

Ah, now there are some "apples of gold" worth savoring.

God Gives the Best Advice

Although it is a whopping generalization with more than a few exceptions, I've observed that men typically like to fix stuff and women like to fix people.

My husband can fearlessly dismantle and repair vehicles, appliances, machines, and even computers, but I believe he'd rather have a root canal without Novacain than try to figure out, or heaven forbid, fix, a person.

I, on the other hand, don't even know how to change the oil in my car, but I'm almost always sure I can steer anyone out of any mess if they ask me ... or even if they don't.

The older I get, though, the more I realize that people almost never want me to fix them (shoooooot) and I'm really not very good at greasing all the cosmic wheels in the universe.

I've been pondering this of late because I've increasingly found myself on the receiving end of the female compulsion to fix people. Due to some frustrating health challenges, I've received boatloads of amateur medical advice from kind folks with good intentions.

Try this ... take that ... be sure not to eat those.

I was gratefully considering all the advice I was receiving until a friend pushed me over the edge with her suggestion to eliminate all sugar and most carbohydrates from my diet.

No sugar and carbohydrates? Why don't I just shave my head and lie down naked on a bed of nails on top of a frosty mountain peak in Tibet? No, thanks. I'd like to keep some life in my life, and a life without chocolate chip cookies and yeast rolls doesn't sound like living to me.

I appreciate the compassionate hearts behind all the advice I've received, but it can certainly be a bit overwhelming to be bombarded with so many suggestions. And now that I know what it feels like to be on the bottom of the good advice pile-on, I think perhaps I should install a flow control on my own fountain 'o wisdom.

Besides, I came up with my own "natural remedy" for my various and assorted maladies—I think I probably just need to rearrange the furniture in our living room. I must've gotten my ying and my yang out of whack, obviously throwing my feng-shui out of balance and thus stifling all the good karma that usually floats around our house.

So if I just move our two couches, all will be right in my universe. Yeah, right.

There's a whole lot of advice floating around out there. Good, evil and just plain kooky. I don't generally mind receiving tips from others, but when it begins to get confusing, I'm thankful I can go back to the sure thing I know and trust—the truth of God, communicated in His word and designed to bless and protect me. Every specific situation I encounter in life is not addressed in the Bible, but there are foundational principles to help me navigate all the waters of my life. And they are not complicated or confusing.

Consider this: When Jesus was asked what the greatest commandments were, He simply said we are to love God and love others

(Matthew 22:36-40). When Jesus was asked how to "work the works of God," He said we are to believe in Him (John 6:28-29). Pretty straight-up stuff.

We like to make it complicated for ourselves and others, but it really shouldn't be. It's not about a thousand rules to keep, herbal remedies, good karma, or eating whole grains and vegetables. It's about living in intimate relationship with the One who made us.

So, here's my advice (oops, there I go again): Seek God and His wisdom. When others serve up some advice, swallow the meat and spit out the bones.

Now, if you'll excuse me, I think I'll go rearrange my couches ... just in case.

(Just kidding.)

God Never Loses His Focus on Us

One of my favorite parts of the movie *Runaway Bride* is when Bob, the football coach fiancé of the main character, Maggie, uses sports psychology to try to train his bride-to-be to overcome her overwhelming fear and actually walk down the wedding aisle and into holy matrimony.

"Focus on Bob ... focus on Bob," he repeatedly tells her, pointing to his eyes and instructing her to concentrate solely on his desperate and determined face.

Boy howdy, I can relate to that poor man. Getting people to focus on me can be pretty darn challenging around my house.

"Focus on Mary Ann ... focus on Mary Ann," I urge my husband, as I share nuggets of information that he truly needs to know.

"Focus on Mom ... focus on Mom," I tell my sons, as I convey vital pearls of maternal wisdom.

Sometimes they focus, sometimes they don't. The problem is, I usually don't know the communication train has derailed until much later when they say, "I don't remember you telling me that."

"But I DID!" I fire back. "I even made you look me in the eyes and focus—and you said you were focusing. Remember?"

They don't.

I sometimes wonder what on earth they are focusing on while my words are bouncing off their ears, but figuring that out would require me to venture into the hinterlands of the male psyche and that's way too scary for me. All I know is that it's quite exasperating to realize you have not been listened to.

I get that same feeling when I'm talking to someone at a social gathering and I realize they are looking around me or over me or through me to someone else they'd rather be talking to. Sometimes I wish I had the nerve to sport out with outrageous comments just to test and confirm my suspicion that they aren't really hearing a word I'm saying.

"Did I tell you that my niece just gave birth to a camel?" I ask.

"Uh huh, that's nice," they mumble, craning their necks to see who's across the room.

"And I used to be six inches taller before I was abducted by aliens in the 8th grade."

"Uh, huh …"

"And I broke up with Kevin Costner to marry my husband."

"Yeah … okay..."

There's nothing like dealing with people to make me appreciate how God deals with me. I never have to wonder if He is distracted. He's not. I never have to wonder if He is perhaps hearing my words but missing my heart. He isn't. He is zeroed in.

In fact, the Bible says His thoughts toward me are "like the sands of the sea" (Psalm 139). Ever tried to count the grains in a handful of sand? How about just a teaspoonful? Now think about the sand on all the beaches in the world. Okay, those are a lot of thoughts …

all about me and my life, and you and your life. We're always on God's mind.

No matter what time of day or night I go to God, He can honestly say to me, "Hey—I was just thinking about you."

I don't know about you, but I find great comfort in that. I don't have to corral God's attention and beg, "C'mon, God, please pay attention to what I'm saying here."

He's already focused, already listening. Hearing every word I say, and all the words I can't.

Let's Talk About Communication ... Group Discussion Questions

1. Can you share any examples of times when words—positive or negative—had a big impact on you?

2. Read Proverbs 6:16-19 and notice the seven things that are an "abomination" to God. Discuss the things listed in this passage that are related to communication. Why do you think these are so important to God?

3. Read Psalm 34:12-13 and discuss how our words affect the quality of our lives and our days.

4. What keeps us from using our words to encourage each other more often?

5. Why does it often seem harder to say positive things than negative things?

6. Should we always offer advice when someone tells us about a problem they are having? Why or why not?

7. What does it communicate to others when they are talking to us and we are not really paying attention to what they are saying? Why are good listeners so rare? How can we become better listeners?

8. What is the best thing to do when you're in the presence of someone who is gossiping?

9. How hard do you think it would be to go a whole day without complaining, criticizing or gossiping? (Want to make a pact to try it this week?)

Dig a Little Deeper ... Individual Study

1. Read Proverbs 18:21–*"Death and life are in the power of the tongue, and those who love it will eat its fruit."*

    ▪ Has anyone ever spoken words to you that were "life-giving"? Explain: _____

    _____

    _____

    _____

    ▪ Have you ever been on the receiving end of words that hurt and felt like "death" to you? Explain: _____

    _____

    _____

    _____

    _____

    ▪ Think about how you speak to others. Are there any ways you regularly try to speak "life" into the lives of people around you? _____

    _____

    _____

    _____

    _____

    ▪ Have you ever said hurtful things to others that probably felt like "death" to them? Explain: _____

    _____

    _____

_____

_____

_____

- Can you think of any time you "ate the fruit" of your words, positive or negative? If so, explain the circumstances: _____

_____

_____

_____

2. Read Proverbs 6:16-19 – *"There are six things which the LORD hates, yes, seven which are an abomination to Him: Haughty eyes, a lying tongue, and hands that shed innocent blood, a heart that devises wicked plans, feet that run rapidly to evil, a false witness who utters lies, and one who spreads strife among brothers."*

  - Which three of these "abominations" are related to communication? (Hint: two are essentially the same, but list them separately anyway.) _____

  _____

  _____

  - What does this imply about the importance God places upon the things we say? _____

  _____

  _____

  _____

3. Read Ephesians 4:29 – *"Let no unwholesome word proceed from your mouth, but only such a word as is good for edification according to the need of the moment, so that it will give grace to those who hear."*

   ▪ The word "unwholesome" comes from the Greek word "sapros," which means "rotten, putrefied, corrupted, worn out, of poor quality, bad, unfit for use, worthless." What kinds of negative speech or communication fit this definition? _____

   _____

   _____

   _____

   _____

   ▪ The word translated as "good" in this verse is from the Greek word "agathos," which means "of good constitution or nature, useful, salutary, pleasant, agreeable, joyful, happy, excellent, distinguished, upright, honorable." What kinds of speech/communication fit this definition? _____

   _____

   _____

   _____

   _____

4. Read the following verses and beside each, write the positive verbal communication we are instructed to engage in:

   ▪ Psalm 37:30 – *"The mouth of the righteous utters wisdom, and his tongue speaks justice."* _____

_____

_____

- Psalm 71:15-17 – *"My mouth shall tell of your righteousness and of Your salvation all day long; for I do not know the sum of them. I will come with the mighty deeds of the Lord God; I will make mention of Your righteousness, Yours alone. O God, You have taught me from my youth, and I still declare Your wondrous deeds."* _____

_____

_____

- Proverbs 15:4 – *"A soothing tongue is a tree of life, but perversion in it crushes the spirit."*

_____

_____

- 1 Peter 3:8-9 – *"To sum up, all of you be harmonious, sympathetic, brotherly, kindhearted, and humble in spirit; not returning evil for evil or insult for insult, but giving a blessing instead; for you were called for the very purpose that you might inherit a blessing."* _____

_____

_____

5. Read Colossians 4:6 – *"Let your speech always be with grace, as though seasoned with salt, so that you will know how you should respond to each person."*

- Consider the following facts about salt and explain how each is a good analogy for positive, godly communication (conversation that is "seasoned with salt"):
- Salt is used to preserve food, like meat:_____
- Salt is used to make food taste better: _____
- Salt makes people thirsty: _____
- Salt is used to melt ice: _____
- Salt is an essential part of the human diet: _____
- In the Old Testament, salt was used in sacrifices made to the Lord (see Leviticus 2:13): _____

  _____

- In the Old Testament, salt was sometimes used to seal covenants (agreements, contracts—see 2 Chronicles 13:5 and Numbers 18:19) _____

  _____

- Salt was sometimes used in the care of newborn babies (see Ezekiel 16:4, and here's a hint to make it relevant to us today: think spiritual "babies") _____

  _____

6. Read the following verses and beside each, write the kind of negative verbal communication we are instructed to avoid:
   - Exodus 22:28 – *"You shall not curse God, nor curse a ruler of your people."* _____

     _____

- Psalm 34:12-13 – *"Who is the man who desires life and loves length of days that he may see good? Keep your tongue from evil and your lips from speaking deceit."* _____

  _____

- Proverbs 18:8 – *"The words of a whisperer are like dainty morsels, and they go down into the innermost parts of the body."* _____

  _____

- Proverbs 29:11 – *"A fool always loses his temper, but a wise man holds it back."* _____

- James 4:11 – *"Do not speak against one another, brethren. He who speaks against a brother or judges his brother, speaks against the law and judges the law; but if you judge the law, you are not a doer of the law but a judge of it."* _____

  _____

- Ephesians 5:4 – *"and there must be no filthiness and silly talk, or coarse jesting, which are not fitting, but rather giving of thanks."* _____

  _____

- Colossians 3:8-10 – *"But now you also, put them all aside: anger, wrath, malice, slander, and abusive speech from your mouth. Do not lie to one another, since you laid aside the old self with its evil practices, and have put on the new self who is being renewed to a true knowledge according to the image of the One who created him ..."* _____

_____

_____

7. In the book of Jude, the author describes ungodly people who infiltrate the church, pretending to be believers. Read the following verse and circle the ungodly characteristics or behaviors that are related to communication:

- Jude 1:16 – *"These are grumblers, finding fault, following after their own lusts; they speak arrogantly, flattering people for the sake of gaining an advantage."*

- Are you surprised that so many of these are related to speech? Why or why not? _____

  _____

  _____

- What does this say about the importance of our words?

  _____

  _____

8. Read Matthew 12:34-35 – *"You brood of vipers, how can you, being evil, speak what is good? For the mouth speaks out of that which fills the heart. The good man brings out of his good treasure what is good; and the evil man brings out of his evil treasure what is evil."*

- According to this verse, what do our words reflect?

  _____

- If you find yourself sinning with your words, what do you need to examine? _____

- Have you ever shocked yourself by saying something you didn't even realize you were thinking or feeling until it came out of your mouth? Explain: _____

  _____

  _____

9. Read James 3:9-11 – *"With it we bless our Lord and Father, and with it we curse men, who have been made in the likeness of God; from the same mouth come both blessing and cursing. My brethren, these things ought not to be this way. Does a fountain send out from the same opening both fresh and bitter water?"*

   - Have you personally experienced the truth of this Scripture— blessing and cursing coming from the same mouth (your own or someone else's)? Explain: _____

     _____

     _____

     _____

     _____

10. Read James 3:2 & 8 – *"For we all stumble in many ways. If anyone does not stumble in what he says, he is a perfect man, able to bridle the whole body as well. ... But no one can tame the tongue; it is a restless evil and full of deadly poison."*

- The word "restless" in verse 8 is from a Greek word "akata-statos," which means "unsettled, unstable, disorderly." Do you ever feel that way about your tongue? Explain: _____

  _____

  _____

  _____

  _____

  _____

- Do these verses encourage you or discourage you (or both)? Why?_____

  _____

  _____

  _____

  _____

  _____

11. Read Philippians 3:12 – *"Not that I have already obtained it or have already become perfect, but I press on so that I may lay hold of that for which also I was laid hold of by Christ Jesus."*

- It's possible, even likely, that at the end of every day, we'll look back and realize that we haven't perfectly controlled our tongues. But, according to what the Apostle Paul has written in the verse above, what should we do when we see that we've fallen short? _____

  _____

  _____

- List one or more specific things you can start doing right NOW to better control your tongue: _____

  _____

  _____

  _____

12. Read James 1:19 – *"This you know, my beloved brethren, but everyone must be quick to hear, slow to speak and slow to anger."*

    - We are commanded in this verse to be quick to _____ and slow to _____.

    - Have you ever known folks you tend to avoid because they talk too much? (Don't name names here—just "yes" or "no")

      _____

    - Do you think there's a chance that others may perhaps be avoiding you because you talk too much? _____

    - What are some characteristics of a good listener? _____

      _____

    - Why are good listeners so rare? _____

      _____

      _____

      _____

13. What have you learned about the importance of communication from this study? _____

    _____

    _____

_____

_____

_____

_____

_____

14. Close this study with a time of prayer. If you have sinned in the area of communication, take time to confess your sins, give thanks for God's forgiveness, and ask Him to help you become a better communicator. You may write out your prayer here if you wish. _____

_____

_____

_____

_____

_____

_____

_____

_____

_____

_____

_____

_____

_____

Microwaves. Fast food. Instant messaging.
Overnight shipping.
We want things when we want them, and
usually that is NOW.
Many of us have developed a serious "wait" problem.
Let's talk about...

WAITING ON GOD

I Have a Wait Problem

I don't do waiting well.

In fact, if waiting were food, I'd stuff it down the garbage disposal.

If it were a car, I'd push it off a cliff.

If it were a dress, I'd sell it in a yard sale ... cheap.

One definition of waiting is "to stay in place in expectation of something." I say it's just pure torture. Oh, I'm good at the expecting part; it's that "staying in place" part that gets me every time.

I remember a week when my car and my body both decided to go on the fritz at the same time, requiring me to spend way too many hours hanging out in various waiting rooms. I hated it. I suppose I could have passed the time reading tacky magazines, but I just couldn't muster up much interest in the newest foolproof way to melt fat while you sleep, or the seven sure signs that your neighbor is a serial killer.

So, I just sat and ... (sigh) ... waited.

"This would be a good time to pray," I thought. "I've been griping about not having enough time to slow down and pray. Well, here's a chunk of time."

Yes, indeed, that was a great idea, but try as I might, I just couldn't seem to lasso my thoughts and quiet my spirit. Waiting doesn't feel peaceful to me—it feels edgy. If I'm sitting in a waiting room, my train of thought flies off the track every time someone comes in, peeks around the corner or strolls by. I'm like a DVD player with the "pause" button pushed, perched in the netherworld between "stop" and "play," ready to be summoned from the waiting room at any second.

In many doctors' offices these days, once you've served out your sentence in the first waiting room, they park you in a second waiting area for awhile. Then they put you in the little exam room and make you wait again. The triple-waiting whammy.

A childhood friend of mine grew up to be an optometrist's assistant. Her gynecologist came in to have his eyes examined and as my friend ushered this doctor into the optometric exam room, she facetiously told him, "Hello, Dr. So-and-so. Take off everything but your socks and cover up with this little paper napkin, while I turn the thermostat down to 50 degrees. The doctor will be in to see you in an hour or so."

My friend was kidding, but she was also reminding this doctor, on behalf of females everywhere, that it's no fun to be left waiting in a cold and barren exam room. (Am I the only one who has resorted to reading the back of hand sanitizer bottles to pass the time while waiting there on that exam table?)

Waiting is especially challenging, I think, for those of us who are members of the drive-through, microwave, overnight-shipping generation, but the Bible indicates that even when life was much slower, waiting was never particularly easy or fun ...

After God promised a baby to senior citizens Abraham and Sarah, the couple had to wait more than two more decades to hold Isaac in their arms.

Moses tended sheep in the desert for 40 years before God came to Him with marching orders to lead the children of Israel to the Promised Land. As we know, that two-week trip ended up taking 40 more years ... after which Moses still didn't get to enter the land.

Jesus waited 30 years to begin his public ministry, working as a carpenter and knowing all the while that He had come to earth to build the kingdom of His Father, not furniture.

Waiting isn't easy. We are, after all, eternal creatures temporarily stranded in time. But the wait will one day be over. When God finally stops the clock, we'll check out of this world. No more feeling like we're stuck in a waiting room filled with old copies of *Field & Stream* magazine.

Those who have placed their faith in Jesus Christ are headed for a glorious new world without deadlines, boredom or anxiety.

And that, my friends, is worth waiting for.

Life's Hassles: Problems or Providence?

Scottish poet Robert Burns got it right: "The best laid schemes of mice and men oft go awry."

I don't know what frustrations Burns was experiencing or observing when he wrote those lines in 1785. I am sure, though, that he wasn't trying to fly to Jamaica for his honeymoon, like my son and his new bride were when they experienced a wee bit of the poet's angst.

Aye, 'tis true—even our most carefully made plans can indeed go awry.

Arriving at the airport to catch a morning flight to paradise, our newlywed son and daughter-in-law were greeted with an announcement that their plane was "broken" (a direct quote).

I don't think "broken" and "plane" should ever be used in the same sentence. I try very hard to pretend that planes can't break.

So, Andy and Janine's first morning together as husband and wife turned out to be one of those frustrating hurry-up-and-wait life experiences. They did eventually get to Jamaica that evening, arriving just ahead of a tropical storm that apparently booked a reservation for the same time … but that's a story for another time.

As for the whole "broken plane" thing, I was sorry their honeymoon plans didn't go according to script, but very, very thankful that the problem was discovered while the plane was still on terra firma.

In fact, when Janine posted a message about their delayed plans on her "Facebook" page (even newlyweds can get bored while waiting in airports), I responded with this message: "Old Chinese proverb say, 'Much better to be stuck in airport than frying on broken prane ... even on honeymoon.'"

The way I see it, there are two ways to look at delays, detours and disappointments: as problems or as providence. Our perspective has everything to do with our belief about ultimate control in this universe.

If we believe that no one is at the helm, then we're doomed to also believe that what happens in our lives and in the world is random. That means we're at the mercy of the whims, mistakes and sins of others and ourselves. Pretty scary.

I may start out feeling quite in control of my destiny today, only to have that control usurped by a toddler who doesn't care about my to-do list, a boss who dumps a new assignment on my desk, a spouse who needs me to squeeze an unexpected errand into my schedule, a bad driver who runs a stop sign, a virus that batters my immune system, a broken plane, or a tropical storm.

But if I believe that there is a very real, personal, wise, good, loving, all-powerful God who has a plan and is in control, then I can rest in His assurance that He is skillfully weaving all the threads of my life together to make a beautiful tapestry.

The backside of that tapestry may look like an ugly tangle of threads and knots with almost no discernible pattern. That's the way life sometimes looks to us, living as we are on this backside of heaven.

But turn that tapestry over, as believers in Christ will get to do one day, and we'll see how God wove all the threads together to make something beautiful.

Delays, detours and disappointments—problems or providence?

I choose providence; I choose God, who promises to ultimately *"work all things together for good to those who love Him and are called according to His purpose."* (Romans 8:28)

His "best laid schemes" never go awry.

"'For I know the plans that I have for you,' declares the LORD, 'plans for welfare and not for calamity to give you a future and a hope....'" (Jeremiah 29:11)

As Squirmy as a Lizard on a Leash

When my boys were little guys, my older son convinced us that he needed an iguana.

Personally, I don't see how "need" and "iguana" could be even remotely linked in any universe, but Ryan had saved his money, so we relented and went iguana shopping. The iguana he picked out was small, which was good. Something that ugly should definitely be small.

My son also bought some iguana accessories, including a leash to hook up to the critter to take him for walks. Yes, that's right. A leash made especially for iguanas. Who knew?

I couldn't quite wrap my brain around the concept of walking an iguana, but I figured it was a guy thing. Part of the quirky male mystique and all that.

So Ryan brought Iggy home and began to hitch him up for their first stroll together. It didn't go well. No, I'd say that maiden voyage was pretty much a disaster.

The little psycho-lizard went nuts, and the stroll turned into a hideous iguana voodoo dance. Iggy had himself a jumping and twisting conniption fit, appearing very much to be trying to hang himself on his leash. (I confess I thought that might not be such a bad thing.)

Ryan tried to convince Iggy that walking on a leash would be fun. Bless his heart, he tried. But Iggy the Spaz was not buying it.

Memories of Iggy returned years later as I was changing the diaper of my visiting granddaughter, a one-year-old bundle of uber-cute energy. We were on the floor and I was having quite a time getting Edda's squirmy bottom into a diaper.

Being a new grandma is forcing me to rehone baby skills that have gotten a bit rusty, but this diaper-changing fiasco wasn't about my lack of practice. It was all about the fact that Edda did not want to slow down for a pit stop.

So she wiggled, writhed, rocked and rolled as I chased, wiped, wrapped and taped. It was quite a show.

Three thoughts came to mind as I wrestled my granddaughter into a Pamper: one was of rodeo calf-roping; the second was the memory of Ryan trying to take that crazy iguana for a walk; and the third was the realization that this must be how God feels when He's trying to change me. Not my diapers, mind you—thankfully, I'm between the two diaper phases of life—but I do need my heart, mind, and life changed from time to time, and sometimes the process is a bit of a calf-roping, iguana-walking, diaper-changing ordeal.

All Ryan wanted to do was to enjoy fellowship with his iguana; all I wanted to do was to bless Edda with a clean diaper; all God wants to do is to lead me into the best possible life and into the deepest possible relationship with Himself, and to grow me up to look more and more like Jesus.

As the Bible says in Romans 8:29: *"For those whom He fore-knew, He also predestined to become conformed to the image of His Son ..."*

And in Philippians 1:6: *"For I am confident of this very thing, that He who began a good work in you will perfect it until the day of Christ Jesus."*

When we sense God trying to change us, the best thing we can do is to be still and let Him. Just let Him. It may be hard, but it's gonna be good. It may not happen as quickly as we'd like, but it will happen, and it will be worth the wait.

Let's Talk About Waiting … Group Discussion Questions

1. What are some situations in the past where you've felt stuck in a "waiting room" (figuratively speaking)? Did you later see the wisdom of God's timing?

2. Can you think of any characters in the Bible who had to wait what seemed like a long time for God to fulfill His promises to them?

3. Read Psalm 37:3-8 and discuss some of the things we're told to do while we're waiting on God and what kind of attitude pleases Him.

4. How does waiting on God test our faith?

5. Have you ever acted like an iguana on a leash while you were waiting for God to do His work? Have you found yourself fretting and panicking as you waited for something to happen, and perhaps made a bad decision as a result?

6. What are some of the characteristics of God that make waiting on Him easier (when we choose to focus on them)?

7. Psalm 27:14 (*New King James Version*) says, *"Wait on the LORD; be of good courage, and He shall strengthen your heart; wait, I say, on the LORD!"* What does God promise to us if we courageously wait on God? Have you ever experienced this promise firsthand?

8. Psalm 31:14-15a says, "But as for me, I trust in You, O LORD, I say, 'You are my God.' My times are in Your hand …"

- Are you currently waiting on God to do something in your life, or in the life of a loved one? Have each group member write down circumstances that are forcing them to wait on God and then have a prayer time to commit (or recommit) these situations into God's hand.

Dig a Little Deeper ... Individual Study

1. Read Psalm 37:3-8 – *"Trust in the LORD and do good; dwell in the land and cultivate faithfulness. Delight yourself in the LORD; and He will give you the desires of your heart. Commit your way to the LORD, trust also in Him, and He will do it. He will bring forth your righteousness as the light and your judgment as the noonday. Rest in the LORD and wait patiently for Him; do not fret because of him who prospers in his way, because of the man who carries out wicked schemes. Cease from anger and forsake wrath; do not fret; it leads only to evildoing."*

- Do you feel like you are currently in a "holding pattern," waiting for God to do something in your life? Explain:

_____

_____

_____

- According to this verse, what are some things you should do while you are waiting? _____

_____

_____

- What connection do you think there could be between fretting and evil, as mentioned in this verse? _____

_____

_____

_____

2. Moses was well acquainted with the concept of waiting. Acts 7:25-30 is a New Testament retelling of part of the story of Moses. Read this passage and answer the questions that follow:

   "And he (Moses) supposed that his brethren understood that God was granting them deliverance through him, but they did not understand. On the following day he appeared to them as they were fighting together, and he tried to reconcile them in peace, saying, 'Men, you are brethren, why do you injure one another?' But the one who was injuring his neighbor pushed him away, saying, 'who made you a ruler and judge over us? You do not mean to kill me as you killed the Egyptian yesterday, do you?' At this remark, Moses fled and became an alien in the land of Midian, where he became the father of two sons. After forty years had passed, an angel appeared to him in the wilderness of Mount Sinai, in the flame of a burning thorn bush."

   - How long was Moses in Midian before God came to him and commanded him to lead the enslaved Hebrews to freedom?

   _____

   - Moses was born a Jew, but was adopted as a baby and raised as a member of the royal family of Egypt. As the passage above indicates, Moses left behind the privileges of royalty and ran for his life, hiding out in the wilderness of Midian. Put yourself in his sandals for a minute. What emotions do you think he might have experienced out there in the Midian wilderness every day before God spoke to him in the burning bush? _____

_____

- Have you ever felt any of those same emotions while waiting for your circumstances to change? Explain: _____

_____

_____

_____

_____

_____

3. Read Acts 16:22-26 – *"The crowd rose up together against them, and the chief magistrates tore their robes off them and proceeded to order them to be beaten with rods. When they had struck them with many blows, they threw them into prison, commanding the jailer to guard them securely; and he, having received such a command, threw them into the inner prison and fastened their feet in the stocks. But about midnight Paul and Silas were praying and singing hymns of praise to God, and the prisoners were listening to them; and suddenly there came a great earthquake, so that the foundations of the prison house*

were shaken; and immediately all the doors were opened and everyone's chains were unfastened."

- Is there any indication that Paul and Silas knew how long they might be stuck in prison? _____

  _____

- Imagine that you are Paul or Silas. You've been stripped, severely beaten and now you're sitting in prison with your feet bound in shackles. You don't know whether you'll be rescued, will have to spend the rest of your life in prison, or be put to death. What emotions might you be experiencing?

  _____

  _____

- What did Paul and Silas do while they were waiting in the prison? _____

  _____

- What do you think enabled them to react that way to their difficult circumstances? _____

  _____

  _____

4. God had promised Abraham that his descendants would be "as numerous as the stars in the sky and as the sand on the seashore." But after many years of trying to have children, Abraham and his wife were still childless, so the couple came up with their own plan. Read the passage below and then answer the questions that follow. (Note: In this passage, God had not yet given

this couple their new names, so they are still referred to as Sarai and Abram)

- Genesis 16:1-4 – *"Now Sarai, Abram's wife, had borne him no children, and she had an Egyptian maid whose name was Hagar. So Sarai said to Abram, 'Now behold, the LORD has prevented me from bearing children. Please go in to my maid; perhaps I will obtain children through her.' And Abram listened to the voice of Sarai. After Abram had lived ten years in the land of Canaan, Abram's wife Sarai took Hagar the Egyptian, her maid, and gave her to her husband Abram as his wife. He went in to Hagar, and she conceived; and when she saw that she had conceived, her mistress was despised in her sight."*

- When God first told Abraham that he would have many, many descendants, how do you think Abraham felt? _____

  _____

  _____

- As years passed and Sarah did not become pregnant, what kinds of thoughts do you think went through the minds of Abraham and Sarah? _____

  _____

- Abraham and Sarah's servant girl, Hagar, gave birth to Ishmael, while Sarah also eventually had a son, Isaac. In Galatians 4:22-31, Ishmael and his mother, Hagar, and Isaac and his mother, Sarah, are said to symbolize slavery versus freedom, man's way versus God's way. The implication is that when we don't wait for God, but instead try to make things happen in our own strength, we may end up in bondage. Do you agree or disagree? _____

_____

_____

_____

_____

_____

- Have you ever gotten tired of waiting on God and taken matters into your own hands to make something happen? _____

_____

_____

_____

- If you answered "yes" above, did your impulsive decision yield any consequences that were later hard to deal with? Explain: _____

_____

_____

_____

5. Waiting on God requires that we trust His timing in our lives. Read the verse below and answer the questions that follow.

- Psalm 145:15-16 – *"The eyes of all look to You, and You give them their food in due time. You open Your hand and satisfy the desire of every living thing."*
- To whom should we look when we have needs?

  _____

- When does God give us what we need? _____

6. Sometimes waiting to see positive results from our efforts makes us weary. Galatians 6:9 says, *"Let us not lose heart in doing good, for in due time we will reap if we do not grow weary."* The Greek word translated "due" in this verse is idios, which means "personal, belonging to oneself"; the Greek word translated "time" is kairos, which means the "exact, opportune, right time." "Due time," then, is the moment that is exactly, personally right for us, as determined by an all-knowing, loving God.
   - Reread Galatians 6:9 (above) and Psalm 145:15-16 (in the preceding question) with that definition of "due time" in mind. Does this shed any new light on God's timing in your life? _____

     _____

     _____

     _____

     _____

7. Isaiah 40:31 says, *"Yet those who wait for the LORD will gain new strength; they will mount up with wings like eagles, they will run and not get tired, they will walk and not become weary."*

- There are some wonderful promises given here to those who wait for (who look for, hope in and expect) the Lord. Fill in the blanks below.
  - *If I wait for the Lord, then ...*
    - I will gain new _____.
    - I will _____ _____ with wings like eagles.
    - I will _____ and not get tired; I will _____ and not become weary.

8. Psalm 27:14 (*New King James Version*) says, *"Wait on the LORD; be of good courage, and He shall strengthen your heart; wait, I say, on the LORD!"*

   - What does God promise to us if we courageously wait on God? _____

   - Have you ever experienced this promise firsthand? _____

     _____

     _____

     _____

     _____

9. Sometimes, even the Lord waits. Read Isaiah 30:18 from the *Amplified Bible: "Therefore the Lord [earnestly] waits [expecting, looking, and longing] to be gracious to you; and therefore He lifts Himself up, that He may have mercy on you and show lovingkindness to you. For the Lord is a God of justice. Blessed [happy, fortunate, to be envied] are all those who [earnestly] wait for Him, who expect and look and long for Him*

[for His victory, His favor, His love, His peace, His joy, and His matchless, unbroken companionship]."

- According to this verse, what is the Lord waiting to do?

  _____

- What are the three words in parentheses after the word "waits" that shed more light on how that word is used in this verse? _____, _____ and

  _____.

- Complete this sentence based on the last part of the verse above: I am blessed if I earnestly _____ for Him, and if I expect and look and _____ for Him (for His victory, His favor, His _____, His _____, His _____ and His matchless, unbroken _____).

10. What have you learned from this study about waiting for God's timing and plan for your life? _____

    _____

    _____

    _____

    _____

    _____

    _____

    _____

11. Psalm 31: 14-15a says, *"But as for me, I trust in You, O LORD, I say, 'You are my God.' My times are in Your hand ..."* Write out

a prayer in the space below, renewing your commitment to wait upon God for His wisdom, direction and action on your behalf.

_____

_____

_____

_____

_____

_____

_____

_____

_____

_____

_____

_____

_____

_____

_____

_____

_____

_____

_____

_____

Fretful? Frazzled? Frenzied?
Yeah, me too. But there's an alternative.
Let's talk about …

PEACE

Peace in the Storm

Pass the doggy Valium, please. I have just endured another episode of my dog's thunderstorm neurosis and I have the claw marks on my leg to prove it. Either he needs medication, or I do.

As a pup, Winston loved to go out and romp in the rain, but now he whimpers, paces, froths, foams, shakes and tries to crawl onto our laps every time a storm blows in. It's pitiful, although apparently not uncommon.

One friend told me her dog always jumps into the bathtub when a storm approaches; another told me that thunder sends her beefy rottweiler scurrying under the covers and transforms him into a whiny, cowering wimp.

A neighbor was visiting recently and described a T.V. show featuring a "pet psychic," a program she watches not because she believes it is legitimate, but because it is so obviously bogus. This bizarre show features a lady who claims to serve as a translator for pets, dead or alive, and their owners.

One episode featured the pet psychic out in a field conversing with a buffalo on behalf of its owner. It seems the buffalo wanted to know if he was going to be moved to a new pasture. The pet whacko … er, I mean psychic … was able to reassure the buffalo that yes, he could look forward to a change of scenery. How nice.

When my neighbor got up to leave after telling me her hilarious pet psychic stories, she paused and silently glared at Winston. She said she was passing on a message from her miniature dachshund.

Actually, when Winston goes berserk during a storm and my efforts to calm him are failing miserably, I might indeed be willing to pay good money to anyone who could communicate this one thing to my dog: "Winston, everything is just fine. You are safe, so relax and enjoy your good life."

I've heard that the phrase "fear not" appears in the Bible 366 times. I've never actually counted them all myself, but if that number is accurate, that means there is a "fear not" for each day of the year (and one for leap year). Do ya think maybe God is trying to tell us something?

Far too often, when adversity blows into my life, I'm like Winston in a storm. God wants very much to reassure me that He is in control and I am safe in His care, but I often don't hear His calming voice because I'm doing my version of Winston's neurotic, frantic rain dance.

The fact is, Winston has nothing to fear when he's inside our house during a storm. He's as safe as he can be. And most of the time, I really have nothing to fear when I'm afraid. It's just a big waste of energy. As Mark Twain said, "I have spent most of my time worrying about things that have never happened."

Jesus didn't do that. In fact, the Bible tells us that Jesus slept soundly through a raging storm that threatened to sink the ship he was snoozing upon. When awakened by his terrified disciples, He simply ordered the wind and waves to be still … and they were. No problemo.

When we pray, God may choose to intervene and calm the craziness around us. But always, He desires to calm the craziness within us. He says, "Peace, be still" to our quivering, fearful hearts. And when we embrace the unsurpassable, incomprehensible, illogical peace of God, it doesn't seem to matter so much how big the waves are or how loud the thunder booms.

Rest for the Weary

I wonder why all the places in this world that promise rest so seldom actually deliver it?

Hotels, for example. Luxurious, undisturbed rest for weary travelers? Maybe, if you are exceedingly lucky or can afford to pay big bucks for your room. But often—at least for budget-conscious peasants like me—these "havens of rest" feature beds that feel like a slabs of slate, AC units that roar like jet engines, slamming doors in the hallways, and never, ever, ever enough towels.

And hospitals? I have the utmost respect and gratitude for folks who work in hospitals, but let's face it, a hospital is NO place to rest. After enduring days and nights of what seem like hourly intrusions, most people would walk through fire to get out of that place so they can get some real rest at home. Take my word for it—it is very surreal, indeed, to be awakened in the wee hours of the night in a medicated fog to find yourself surrounded by strangers instructing you to blow as hard as you can into a plastic thing to make sure your lungs are functioning well. It makes all those alien abduction stories seem a bit more plausible.

I've read where prisoners of war are sometimes tortured by being kept awake for extended periods of time, then allowed to doze off, only to be abruptly awakened again. Sounds like a hospital stay to me.

What about all the other places in the world that promise rest, but come up woefully short?:

RESTrooms—who wants to lounge and linger in there? Yuck.

RESTaurants—who can relax when the sticky kid behind you is wiping ketchup all over the back of your booth?

REST homes—whose turn is it to pretend they are Teddy Roosevelt or Queen Elizabeth today?

I've had to endure more than a few rounds of post-surgical "rest" and you know what? It didn't feel restful at all. While my body was still, my mind was in high gear. I envisioned weeks of peacefully watching old movies and reading good books; instead, I fretted about all the things I wasn't getting done. And fretting is decidedly not restful.

Everything around us usually seems to conspire to make rest hard to come by, but I'm finally beginning to understand that there is, indeed, a place of spiritual, emotional and mental rest I can find when life gets noisy and challenging. It's found in the presence of God and the way in is simple: prayer.

Talking to God about all the things that threaten to steal my peace—worries, burdens and frustrations—transports me into the rest of God and allows me to experience the truth of *Isaiah 26:3:* *"You (God) will keep in perfect peace him whose mind is steadfast, because he trusts in You."*

I give Him my worries—He gives me His peace; I give Him my confusion—He gives me His wisdom; I give Him my weakness—He gives me His strength; I place my faith in Him—and He gives me His rest. It's quite the deal.

We don't need to go anywhere in order to get the rest, peace and quiet our hearts desperately long for. Those precious things are only a prayer away.

Jesus says, *"Are you tired? Worn out? Burned out on religion? Come to me. Get away with me and you'll recover your life. I'll show you how to take a real rest. Walk with me and work with me – watch how I do it. Learn the unforced rhythms of grace. I won't lay anything heavy or ill-fitting on you. Keep company with me and you'll learn to live freely and lightly."* – Matthew 11:28-30 *(The Message)*

Take Time to Quiet Down

Can anybody out there say, "Brrrrrrrrrrrrr"?

It's been crazy cold here in South Carolina. Like Yankee, freeze-your-nostrils-shut cold.

It has me wondering if maybe, just maybe, a white Christmas might not be totally out of the question around here.

Wow—wouldn't that be something? Convenience stores packed with frantic, last-minute holiday shoppers AND the milk-and-bread snow crowd.

I experienced a few white Christmases growing up in Indiana. They were nice, even though the price tag usually included tolerating dirty little mountains of snow in parking lots and on roadsides until the spring thaw. But yes, a white Christmas was a bit magical.

If I could order up a Christmas snow here in South Carolina, I surely would, because this would be a wonderful place for that to happen. Snowfalls here are perfect—beautiful, fun and gone before they get grungy.

Travel woes notwithstanding, there's a lot to like about an occasional good snowfall. I especially appreciate the amazing quiet that settles in as snow begins to pile up. Life stops and schedules change. God gently lays a blanket of insulation over the land and over life for just a little while.

When I go outside and traipse through the snowy woods around our house, it's almost like I've been transported to another dimension—Narnia or Wonderland or Oz. Everything seems different, serene, pristine.

I feel permission to gear down, simmer down, and quiet down.

You may think this sounds crazy, but that's how I sometimes feel when I worship God. I mean really worship Him. Mindlessly going through the religious motions doesn't count. Mentally compiling my Walmart list while my lips are singing or praying doesn't count.

But when I'm really engaging, really thinking about what I'm singing and praying, sometimes I become keenly aware that I'm in the very presence of God Almighty. I glimpse His greatness and majesty, but I also sense His tender smile, like a proud papa at a piano recital. His unfathomable love wraps around me and at least for a little while, I am at peace.

I gear down, simmer down, quiet down inside.

I believe worship blesses God; I know worship blesses us.

I heard a story about a father and his young son who were riding on an elevator and as it stopped on various floors to pick up passengers, the little boy got squeezed toward the back. Obviously, his view wasn't very good with all those big-people keisters directly in his line of sight.

Finally, the boy held out his arms and yelled, "Pick me up, Daddy! I don't like the way things look down here!"

I understand that.

Pick me up, God! I don't like the way things look down here.

When I really worship, when I take time to behold God—His bigness and tenderness, His truth and grace, His power and mercy—it's like He picks me up and suddenly, everything looks different.

"…fears are stilled and strivings cease," one song describes it.

"…in His presence, all things are new" and "…heaven and earth become one," another says.

When I worship God, my nagging worries are muted and my heart can finally get out-in-the-snow quiet.

"Be still and know that I am God," He says. (Psalm 46:10)

"Come to Me … and I will give you rest," He says. (Matthew 11:28)

Worship reminds me who God is … and who is God. It reminds me that nothing is too hard for the One who created it all.

"You will keep in perfect peace those whose minds are steadfast, because they trust in You." – Isaiah 26:3

Let's Talk About Peace ... Group Discussion Questions

1. It's not always clear what someone means when they say they want peace. To some, peace simply means the absence of conflict—in other words, they just don't want anyone to be mad at them personally, or they want our country to avoid war with other nations. *Shalom* is a Hebrew word that is usually translated into English as *peace*. In fact, one of the biblical names of God is "Jehovah Shalom"—God is our peace. But the definition of *shalom* encompasses much more than just the absence of conflict. It also means completeness, wholeness, health, peace, welfare, safety, soundness, tranquility, prosperity, perfectness, fullness, rest, harmony, and the absence of agitation or discord.

   ▪ In light of this more complete definition, how would you respond to someone who says, "I can have peace without having a relationship with God."?

2. What most frequently causes you to lose your peace or to feel anxious?

3. What do you think it means to "rest in God"?

4. Do you ever worry about things that people who live in Third World countries would probably consider "luxury worries"? Can you think of any examples?

5. In what ways do we tend to unnecessarily complicate our lives and increase the stress and "noise" in our lives?

6. Consider Mark Twain's quote: "I have spent most of my time worrying about things that have never happened." Can you relate to that? Can you share any examples from your own life?

7. When we are frequently anxious, worried, and fretful, what do you think that communicates to God and to others who may be watching us? (Co-workers, family members, friends, etc.)

8. Read Matthew 6:25-34. Why do we find it so difficult to simply believe and live out the truth in this passage?

9. Read 2 Corinthians 10:5. What does it mean practically for us to "take every thought captive to the obedience of Christ"? Why is this important if we want to experience more peace in our lives?

10. Read Isaiah 26:3-4 and discuss these questions: What does it mean to have a steadfast mind? What are some practical things we can do to keep our minds fixed on the Lord?

11. Read Isaiah 43:2-3 and discuss these questions: Do these verses promise that we will never have to go through the "fire" or the "deep waters"? What is promised here? Why should that bring us peace? Why doesn't it sometimes?

12. Discuss the relationship between worship, prayer and peace.

Dig a Little Deeper ... Individual Study

1. It's not always clear what someone means when they say they want peace. To some, peace simply means the absence of conflict—in other words, they just don't want anyone to be mad at them personally, or they want our country to avoid war with

other nations. *Shalom* is a Hebrew word that is usually translated into English as *peace*. In fact, one of the biblical names
of God is "Jehovah Shalom"—God is our peace. But the definition of *shalom* encompasses much more than just the absence of
conflict. It also means completeness, wholeness, health, peace,
welfare, safety, soundness, tranquility, prosperity, perfectness,
fullness, rest, harmony, and the absence of agitation or discord.

- In light of this more complete definition, how would you
  respond to someone who says, "I can have peace without
  having a relationship with God."? _____

  _____

  _____

  _____

  _____

  _____

  _____

2. What kinds of situations cause you to worry and feel anxious?

  _____

  _____

  _____

  _____

3. Read Matthew 8:24-27 – "*And behold, there arose a great
   storm on the sea, so that the boat was being covered with the
   waves; but Jesus Himself was asleep. And they came to Him
   and woke Him, saying, 'Save us, Lord; we are perishing!' He*

said to them, 'Why are you afraid, you men of little faith?' Then He got up and rebuked the winds and the sea, and it became perfectly calm. The men were amazed, and said, 'What kind of a man is this, that even the winds and the sea obey Him?'"

- Imagine that you are on the boat with Jesus and His disciples. A storm is raging around you and it looks like the boat is going to go under, but Jesus is taking a nap. What emotions do you think you might be experiencing? _____

  _____

  _____

- Why wasn't Jesus as frantic as His disciples? _____

  _____

  _____

  _____

- The absolute authority of Jesus is displayed in this passage. Over what does Jesus demonstrate authority? _____

  _____

- When you realize the scope of Jesus' authority and power, how does that make you feel about trusting Him when you are facing a tough situation? _____

  _____

4. Read Isaiah 26:3-4 – *"The steadfast of mind You will keep in perfect peace, because he trusts in You. Trust in the LORD forever, for in GOD the LORD, we have an everlasting Rock."*

- The dictionary defines "steadfast" as "fixed or unchanging." What are some practical things you can do to keep your mind fixed on the Lord? _____

- What will God give you if you trust Him and keep your mind fixed on Him? _____

_____

5. Read 2 Corinthians 10:5 – *"We are destroying speculations and every lofty thing raised up against the knowledge of God, and we are taking every thought captive to the obedience of Christ."*

- Rewrite this verse in your own words: _____

_____

_____

_____

- What kinds of anxious thoughts do you sometimes have that may fall under the category of "speculations and every lofty thing raised up against the knowledge of God"? _____

_____

_____

_____

_____

6. Read Isaiah 41:10 – *"Do not fear, for I am with you; do not anxiously look about you, for I am your God. I will strengthen you, surely I will help you, surely I will uphold you with My righteous right hand."*

- God gives a simple reason here why you should not fear or "anxiously look about you." He says, "I am _____ you."

- Obviously, God's presence with us should be enough to blow away all of our worries...but for most of us, sometimes it isn't. Why not? _____

   _____

   _____

7. Read Philippians 4:6-7 – *"Be anxious for nothing, but in every-thing by prayer and supplication with thanksgiving let your requests be made known to God. And the peace of God, which surpasses all comprehension, will guard your hearts and your minds in Christ Jesus."*

   - According to this verse, what should you be anxious about?

      _____

   - What should you pray about? _____

   - When you present your requests to God, what attitude should you have as you pray? _____

      _____

   - What are the duties of someone employed as a guard (think of all kinds of guards)? _____

      _____

      _____

   - In what ways, then, does God's peace "guard" your heart and mind? _____

      _____

- Have you ever experienced supernatural peace in the midst of very stressful circumstances? _____

_____

_____

_____

_____

_____

_____

8. Read Isaiah 43:2-3a – *"When you pass through the waters, I will be with you; and through the rivers, they will not overflow you. When you walk through the fire, you will not be scorched, nor will the flame burn you. For I am the LORD your God, the Holy One of Israel, your Savior ..."*

- You may never have to literally pass through waters, rivers or fire, but what are some of the challenges you face that threaten to steal your peace? _____

_____

_____

- Do these verses promise that you will never have to go through the "waters, rivers or fire"? _____

_____

- What do they promise? _____

_____

- What does that mean to you personally? _____

_____

_____

_____

9. What have you learned about peace from this study? _____

_____

_____

_____

_____

_____

_____

10. Close this study in prayer, asking God to show you anything going on in your life that is causing you anxiety. As something comes to mind, ask God to take care of that person or situation, show you if there is anything He wants you to do regarding that person or situation, and replace your anxiety with His supernatural peace. You may write your prayer below, if you wish.

_____

_____

_____

_____

_____

_____

_____

_____

_____

Fake plants. Fake eyelashes. Fake jewelry.
Fake, fake, fake.
It might be all around us, but it should never describe us.
Let's talk about…

BEING REAL

Don't Clean When a Tornado is Coming

We're probably all familiar with the things we're supposed to do and not do if a tornado is approaching...

- ❖ Go to the lowest and most interior part of a building and hunker down in a crouched position, preferably with a mattress covering your person ... unless, of course, you have a water bed, in which case you are advised to skip the mattress thing.

- ❖ If you're in a mobile home, for Pete's sake, get out—everybody knows they are twister magnets.

- ❖ Do not stand in front of windows with your video camera, no matter how much you crave 30 seconds of fame on the Weather Channel.

- ❖ Do not imagine for one skinny minute that your vehicle can outrun a tornado, even if you are in a 4-wheel drive macho truck with a gun rack, go-faster lights on top, and Yosemite Sam mud flaps.

- ❖ Get out of your vehicle and lie down in a ditch, paying no attention to the slime oozing out of that discarded trash bag next to your face.

Please note that "frantically clean your house" does NOT appear on the tornado preparedness list, although, for some crazy reason, that's exactly what I did one time.

If I might explain …

We're basement people, my husband and I. You see, when it comes to house foundations, you've got your basement people and your slab people and your crawl space people. We are most definitely basement people, so when we built our house, we built it with a basement, which is a bit of an aberration down here in the South.

One unanticipated responsibility that comes with having a basement is that we are now the official storm shelter for our neighborhood. When threatening weather knocks on the door, so do the neighbors.

Earlier this year, a tornado warning was issued for our area and the neighbors understandably came calling. We had just finished supper when the phone began to ring. We didn't even realize a tornado warning had been issued. After all, who needs a weather radio if you have the only basement in the 'hood and your neighbors have a healthy fear of storms?

So, what did I do when I found out a twister had been spotted in our area? Without even consciously thinking about it, I found myself frantically trying to tidy up the kitchen.

With warning sirens going off and neighbors filing down the stairs to our basement, I remained upstairs, cleaning like a crazy woman. It was as if some kind of bizarre primal housekeeping urge possessed me, causing me to subconsciously think, "If our house gets blown away, by golly, the pieces they find will be clean."

What was I thinking—that dying with a dish sponge clutched in my hand would qualify me for domestic sainthood?

"What a woman—she was scrubbing to the bitter end."

Why on earth, under those circumstances, did I care whether or not my kitchen looked good?

But, let's get serious here —don't we sometimes, or even often, do the same thing in our spiritual lives? We become obsessed with making sure our lives appear nice and tidy to others, even when a storm is roaring through and our hearts are being blown to smithereens.

"How ya doin'?" someone asks as we cruise through the church lobby.

"Oh, just fine," we lie, while our minds, hearts and spirits are buckling from the strain of marriage problems, catastrophic health issues, rebellious kids, unemployment, loneliness or mounting debt. We entertain doubts and disappointments we're afraid to even whisper to another human being, let alone to God.

The Pharisees were really good at trying to keep up appearances back in Jesus' day. And Jesus hated it. In fact, He called them "whitewashed tombs." Talk about not mincing words.

Read through the Gospels and you'll quickly discover that Jesus is always more concerned about what's going on inside of us than what we look like on the outside.

If you have some storms brewing in your life right now, don't waste time and energy trying to look like you've got it all together. Don't clean the kitchen if a tornado is upon you.

Be honest. Most especially talk to Jesus about what's going on and let Him be what He so desperately wants to be – "a very present help in time of trouble" … the only real refuge in a storm.

Nobody Else's Shoes Will Fit

Like a moth to the flame, I seem to be instinctively drawn to newspaper articles that set off my bizarrometer. In light of that, I give you the following true story: A 33-year-old woman in Wisconsin was charged with felony identity theft for stealing her 15-year-old daughter's identity. Why? So she could—get this—join the cheerleading squad.

Okay, let's all pause here and take a deep, cleansing breath.

When I read this article, I didn't know whether to laugh or cry. The poor daughter in this story will undoubtedly become a cash cow for a professional counselor. Let's hope she has a "buy one/get one free" coupon and takes her mom with her.

A woman who wants so desperately to be a high school cheerleader that she tries to impersonate her daughter? Puh-leeze. Even gallons of Oil of Delay can't cover up 33 years of living, and precious few 30-somethings can pull off back flips and splits like a nimble teen.

How does someone live with a hormonal teenage daughter and think, even for a moment, "Gee, I want to be you!"?

Why not just ask to be strapped into a roller coaster for a seven-year ride?

I squeezed everything I could from my teen years, but I have no desire to get on that ride again.

Had she succeeded in her scheme to become a teenager again, I'm pretty sure this mom would have been sorely disappointed. As with so many things in this world, the concept is better than the reality. That's always the case when we try to act out roles not written for us.

We've probably all done it at one time or another—wanted to be someone else, look like someone else, have talents like someone else, attract attention and acclaim like someone else, have a house like someone else, a job like someone else, a family like someone else.

This woman just pathetically and publicly walked into a trap that can snag any of us if we get so obsessed with what we want that we become blind to all we have.

God gives you grace to be the person He has created you to be, not a copy of anyone else. No one else's shoes are quite as comfy or their paths quite as smooth as they may seem.

God does have a new identity for each of us, but not one that is stolen. When you place your life in His hands, you receive the identity of Jesus Christ, and He sets about re-creating you into the uniquely best "you" that you can possibly be. The character of Christ wrapped in your distinctive, sanctified personality, with all its gifts and quirks.

Forget pep rallies, pompoms, or anything else you've missed or lost along the way. God has something much better for you right here, right now. Trust me—it's something to cheer about.

194

"...When I was woven together in the depths of the earth, Your eyes saw my unformed body. All the days ordained for me were written in Your book before one of them came to be." (Psalm 139:15b-16)

"For we are God's workmanship, created in Christ Jesus to do good works, which God prepared in advance for us to do." (Ephesians 2:10)

God Wants the Real Thing

Yard art is a curious thing. If your front yard is adorned with one of those wooden cutouts made to look like the hind end of a large woman bending over, please don't take offense, but seriously, what are you thinking? I mean, do you want passersby to think that is YOU out there pulling weeds with your behonkus on display?

And while I'm at it, what's up with putting plastic chickens in the front yard? Real or plastic, I've never thought chickens enhance a home's curb appeal.

Maybe I never developed a healthy appreciation for yard art because I didn't see much of it in my neighborhood during my formative years. But I was certainly exposed to the genre when I visited my grandparents, who lived in a small town where many yards featured large, colored, shiny balls on concrete pedestals.

"Got one of those shiny ball things for your yard yet? Got us one last Tuesday," one friend might have said to another down at the feed-and-seed store. Before long, maybe a wave of yard-art peer pressure rolled through town and the shiny balls started appearing everywhere.

I witnessed a more current and bizarre display of this phenomena recently on a drive up to northern Greenville County, South Carolina. My husband and I ventured up that way to pick up a humongous, rednecky truck that my husband bought ... which is a whole other column screaming to be written. Winding our way up into the Blue Ridge foothills, we passed one pasture, then another, and then another that had life-size cow statues in them.

Yeah, that's right. Fake cows with large horns, just standing there in pastures, looking out at the road, big as you please. I did a double-take each time I saw one and it took me a moment to figure out that the cows were fake. But yes, indeed, they were.

I had never seen even one of these statues in a pasture before, let alone four of them along a short stretch of road. Heaven knows how many counterfeit cows were on display around them thar parts.

I could only guess that some store must have been running a special on bovine statuary — a deal too good to pass up, evidently. I wondered if the statues were supposed to be aesthetically pleasing or if they served some other, mysterious, higher purpose.

You know what bothers me about this? About cow statues, plastic chickens, and wooden bending-over fat ladies? They're fake. And on the whole, I don't like fake.

Yard art is no big deal, so if you enjoy it, go for it. It's your yard. But we mustn't let fake creep into our hearts, our words or our lives.

Jesus got really ticked off at the religious phonies of His day.

Sadly, people like that are still around. They are parked on church pews every Sunday, right alongside folks who truly love and want to follow Jesus Christ with all their heart, mind, soul and strength. Like those cows in the pasture, at first glance it may be hard to tell the plastic from the real, but sooner or later, it shows. Oh yes, it shows.

Make no mistake — God wants real.

"Those who worship must worship in spirit and truth," He says. (John 4:24)

I didn't think anything could look sillier than plastic cows and chickens, but come to think of it, something does — plastic Christians. Let's be real.

Let's Talk About Being Real ... Group Discussion Questions

1. Is it hard for you to let others see that you have problems in your life? Why do you think that is a struggle for many Christians?

2. Why do so many Christians have a hard time being content with the personalities, gifts and talents God has given them?

3. What are the dangers of comparing ourselves to one other?

4. Discuss the news article about the woman who stole her daughter's identity. What values in our culture might encourage this kind of bizarre behavior?

5. At any point in your life, have you ever wanted to be someone else?

6. Can you now look back and appreciate some of the personality traits or gifts that you used to dislike about yourself?

7. In what ways are Christians tempted to "fake" their faith? How can we perhaps change the culture and atmosphere of the church so that Christians don't feel like they need to fake it?

8. Discuss the characteristics of a genuine Christian.

9. Read Proverbs 31:30 and Jeremiah 9:23-24 and discuss the difference between the character traits advocated in these verses and the traits valued by our culture.

10. A popular prayer titled, "The Serenity Prayer," reads as follows: *"God grant me the strength to accept the things I cannot change; courage to change the things I can; and wisdom to*

know the difference." Discuss the kinds of things we can and cannot change about ourselves.

11. Do you spend a lot of time, energy and resources trying to fight or change things about yourself or your life that you really can't change?

Dig a Little Deeper ... Individual Study

1. What do you find most personally challenging about being honest? _____

_____

_____

2. Are you going through any struggles or having any problems right now that you are afraid to talk about because you want others to think your life is nice and tidy? (yes or no) _____.
   If so, what are they? _____

_____

_____

3. Read Matthew 23:27: *"Woe to you, scribes and Pharisees, hypocrites! For you are like whitewashed tombs which on the outside appear beautiful, but inside they are full of dead men's bones and all uncleanness."*

   ▪ Why do you think Jesus spoke so sharply to the religious leaders of his day? _____

_____

_____

- What does Jesus' tone here say about His passion regarding hypocrisy in the church? _____

  _____

  _____

  _____

4. Have you ever had a personal, negative experience with "fake" Christians? If so, explain the situation and the affect it had on you: _____

   _____

   _____

   _____

   _____

5. Do you ever find yourself feeling jealous of the physical traits, talents or personality traits you see in others? Are there certain traits or talents that especially tend to make you jealous? _____

   _____

   _____

   _____

6. Take a moment to step back and imagine what God probably thinks about our culture's obsession with youth, beauty and popularity. What do you think He would say about it all to those who profess faith in Jesus Christ? _____

   _____

   _____

   _____

7. Read the following verses and answer the questions below:

- Proverbs 31:30 – *"Charm is deceitful and beauty is vain, but a woman who fears the LORD, she shall be praised."*

- Jeremiah 9:23-24 – *"Thus says the LORD, 'Let not a wise man boast of his wisdom, and let not the mighty man boast of his might, let not a rich man boast of his riches; but let him who boasts boast of this, that he understands and knows Me, that I am the LORD who exercises lovingkindness, justice and righteousness on earth; for I delight in these things,' declares the LORD."*

- List the attributes found in these verses that are INFERIOR to fearing and knowing God:_____

_____

_____

_____

- How does the message of these verses run contrary to the message we usually receive in our culture? _____

_____

_____

_____

- Do you invest more in your relationship with God or in trying to increase your beauty, position and/or riches? Explain: ___

_____

_____

_____

- What can you change about your life and your daily routine to reflect the priority encouraged in these verses? _____

  _____

  _____

  _____

  _____

8. Think of your life as divided into external things (outward circumstances) and internal things (personality or "heart" things). List items under the following headings:

   - External circumstances and traits I cannot change about myself or my life: _____

     _____

     _____

   - External circumstances and traits I could change about myself or my life: _____

     _____

     _____

   - Internal traits (personality traits, talents) I cannot change about myself: _____

     _____

     _____

   - Internal traits I could (with God's help) change about myself:

     _____

     _____

     _____

9. A popular prayer, called "The Serenity Prayer," reads as follows: *"God grant me the strength to accept the things I cannot change; courage to change the things I can; and wisdom to know the difference."* Pray through the lists you just made above, asking God to help you accept what you cannot change about your life and to give you the courage and wisdom to allow Him to help you change the things you perhaps need to change. If you'd like, you can write out your prayer on the lines below:

_____

_____

_____

_____

_____

_____

_____

_____

_____

_____

_____

10. One key to being content with the "unchangeable" things about ourselves is realizing that God uniquely created us to be essential parts of a "body"—the body of Christ, which is His church. Read 1 Corinthians 12:4-20 and answer the following questions:

- v. 7 – To whom is the "manifestation of the Spirit" given? _____ Does that include you? _____
- v. 11 – Who decides what gifts will be given to believers? _____
- v. 7. – What is the purpose of your gifts? _____ _____
- v. 15-16 – Are your gifts any less important than anyone else's in your church? _____
- v. 18 – Does God give gifts to believers in a random, thoughtless, haphazard way? _____
- How does it hurt the "body" (church) when we wish we could do what other "parts" (members) are doing? _____

_____

_____

_____

_____

11. Read Philippians 3:12 – *"Not that I have already obtained it or have already become perfect, but I press on so that I may lay hold of that for which also I was laid hold of by Christ Jesus."*

- Do we have to wait until we are perfect in order to allow others to see what we're really like? _____
- Instead of focusing on the fact that he wasn't perfect yet, what did Paul say he concentrated on? _____

_____

- In what ways should you be "pressing on" in your life?

  _____

  _____

  _____

12. Read Philippians 1:6 – *"For I am confident of this very thing, that He who began a good work in you will perfect it until the day of Christ Jesus."*
    - Who is the One who works in you? _____
    - What does this verse promise? _____
    - Does God ever put us "out to pasture" and stop working in our lives? _____

13. Has this study changed any of your ideas or fears about being real? _____

    _____

    _____

    _____

    _____

    _____

    _____

    _____

    _____

    _____

    _____

    _____

It's not about IF we trust, because we do; it's about WHO we trust.
God's resumé is infinitely more impressive than anyone else's.
Let's talk about...

TRUST

Let God Do the Flying

My pastor tells the story of a man who was nervous about his first flight on an airplane. After he had safely arrived at his destination, this fellow was asked how he liked his plane trip. "Oh, it was okay," he said, "but I never did put my whole weight on it."

I understand that. I don't have to fly often, but when it's the only reasonable way to get from here to there, I do it. But I don't like it. In fact, I believe I'd have to rank it alongside root canals, colonoscopies and shopping for swimsuits on my don't-wanna-do list.

Don't bother to quote safety statistics to me. I know in my head that flying is actually safer than driving a car, but my head isn't the only part of me boarding that plane. And besides, when I think about something going wrong in a car, I can usually imagine the possibility that I might emerge unscathed. Ain't so when you're 30,000 feet in the air. All the possibilities are worse than awful.

Please don't try to convince me that flying is comfortable, either. Unless you're traveling first class (which I never do) or stopped growing at the age of eight (which I certainly didn't), you're likely to be wedged in your seat tighter than a tater in its skin. The only upside there is that if the plane hits a stretch of turbulence, your nerves may be shaken up, but your hips won't budge.

And speaking of turbulence, well, don't even get me started. I can recall one flight where the ride got so bumpy that I fully expected to look out my window and see the rivets pop out of the wings on that plane. Every hitch in a plane's giddy-up has me calling out to Jesus, convinced I will be meeting Him face to face sooner rather than later.

My husband flies more often than I do and seems to be quite casual about placing his life in the hands of total strangers—the engineers who design these gravity-defying machines, the mechanics who make sure the rivets stay in the wings, the pilots who are supposed to get them where they're going, and the air traffic controllers who direct the aerial ballet around major jetports. But try as I might, I just can't seem to make myself relax and "put my full weight" on those planes. It's almost like I think that my elevated stress level is keeping the aircraft aloft—that the engines are propelled by a mixture of jet fuel and my adrenaline.

I know folks whose spiritual lives are like my plane rides. They've got enough religion to make 'em miserable, but not enough to do 'em any good, as the old saying goes. They're on their way to heaven, but they sure aren't enjoying the trip. Know why? They're afraid to put their full weight on God. They trust Him in some ways, but not in all ways; they give Him pieces of their lives, but not every part; they let Him see the tidy places in their hearts, but constantly fear He will wander off to those dark closets and rooms they are trying so hard to hide.

It's really foolish for me to stay tense throughout a plane flight when I could be enjoying the scenery or taking a nap. Jesus did that, you know, on a boat in the middle of a violent storm. His disciples were going nuts and He was snoozing away.

How could He do that? Here's how: He'd put all His weight on the faithfulness of His Father, whose love and power are absolutely perfect.

I may never really trust airplanes, but come what may, I can certainly trust the One who holds my life in His hands. There are lots of things in this life that I can't, and shouldn't, put my whole weight on—things unworthy of my trust. But God is not one of those things.

He's good and His plans for me are good. Knowing that, maybe next time I fly, I'll just sit back, take a nap and let Him keep the rivets in the wings. I could use the break.

It Could Happen Tomorrow

It was enough to send paranoid, anxious souls scrambling for their nerve pills ...

"A killer tornado could devastate Dallas, a category five hurricane could wipe out New York City, an earthquake could flatten L.A., a tsunami could wash the Pacific Northwest into the sea. It hasn't happened yet, but it COULD happen TOMORROW," warned the doomy, gloomy announcer.

It was a clip promoting a series on the Weather Channel and I heard it over and over every morning when I tuned in for my "Local on the 8s" forecast.

It was starting to mess with my head, I think. It wasn't good to start out every day imagining all the ways the sky might fall in on me. It COULD happen tomorrow. Or today, for that matter. Maybe even in the next five minutes.

Well, sure it could.

A meteor could land on my house; I could be abducted by aliens again (okay, just kidding about the "again" part—I wanted to see if you were paying attention). No doubt about it—this world can be a scary place.

The Bible certainly doesn't sugarcoat the grim realities of life on a fallen planet.

Ask the folks of Sodom and Gomorrah about what could happen tomorrow … oops, wait, you can't—they got fried by fire and brimstone.

Or, okay, ask Job, the Donald Trump of his day. One day he was enjoying a life of luxury; the next, he lost nearly everything but his whiny wife and finger-pointing friends.

Or Joseph. One day he was strutting around in the beautiful robe his daddy had given him; the next, his jealous brothers threw him into a pit and then sold him to slave traders.

Sudden disasters do happen. But you know what? The Bible also records a whole lot of GOOD things that happened just as suddenly …

Moses had been hiding in the wilderness for 40 years, assuming he would spend the rest of his once-glamorous life tending sheep. Then, SUDDENLY, God appeared in a burning bush and spoke to this fugitive prince-turned-shepherd, transforming the life of Moses into an epic adventure.

And speaking of shepherds, as the youngest kid in his family, David got assigned the dirty, lonely job of tending sheep. One day he was SUDDENLY called in from the fields and before he could shake the wool off his robe, the lad was anointed king. Quite a promotion.

Mary was a young peasant girl living in an obscure village, probably planning an obscure life with her obscure fiancé … until the angel Gabriel SUDDENLY popped in one day and announced that she would give birth to the Son of God. Nothing obscure about that.

A man was lying by the pool of Bethesda, along with others who were "sick, blind, lame, and withered" (John 5:3), trying unsuccessfully to be the first person to slide into the pool whenever the angel stirred the waters. Only the first person in got healed, and he'd never won that race. How many times had this man tried, failed and endured another day of frustrated misery? We don't know, but we do know he had been ill for 38 years, which is a LONG time. But one day, SUDDENLY, everything changed when Jesus walked up and instantly gave him the thing he'd been dreaming of for nearly four decades—health and wholeness.

None of these folks anticipated the wondrous things that happened to them. One moment life was normal; in an instant, everything changed.

And so it is with us. It COULD happen. Your sickness could be healed; you could get that job you've been praying for; your prodigal child could return home.

God calls Himself "the God of all hope" (Romans 15:13) for a reason. Nothing is impossible with Him. Nothing.

Everybody Trusts Something

Everybody lives by faith..

Don't believe me?

Your alarm goes off and you roll out of bed—the bed you trusted all night long to hold you up. You probably weren't too nervous about whether that bed was going to cave in and send you crashing to the floor, were you?

It's dark outside, so how do you know your alarm clock is waking you up at the right time? You don't know; you trust.

You stumble to the bathroom and get a drink of water. How do you know that water is really safe to drink? You don't know; you trust.

You sit down to eat a bowl of cereal. How do you know your Shredded Wheat is really shredded wheat? You didn't see it being made. Could be shredded cardboard or tree bark, for all you know. But you trust.

You get in your car to go to work. What if the brakes don't work? What if the tires were made out of defective rubber? How do you know that was really gasoline you put in your tank yesterday? You don't know; you trust.

And what about all those other drivers out there on the road? One of them might be feeling suicidal today. Some of them may have failed their driving tests. It's likely that at least one of them is texting their BFF while cruising toward you. You don't know anything about them, but you trust (and buckle your seatbelt).

You get on an elevator to ride up to your office. How do you know the elevator is safe? You can't see the cables or hydraulic thingies that are hoisting you up 20 stories. You don't know; you can't see; you trust.

The day has just begun and you've had to muster the faith of Moses to even get to work.

If you've ever flown on an airplane, taken medicine, eaten in a restaurant, undergone a medical procedure, or deposited your paycheck in a bank, you have faith.

I'll say it again: Everybody lives by faith.

The atheist has faith that there is no God. I believe there is, that He created the heavens and the earth, and that He calls us to live in glorious relationship with Him.

The unbeliever trusts that Jesus was a lunatic or a liar. I believe that Jesus is exactly who He says He is, and that He will do all He promises to do.

The skeptic trusts that Jesus was not resurrected from the dead. I believe He was, based on His own words, as well as the historical testimony of eyewitnesses who saw the empty tomb and the risen Christ. (By the way, many of those eyewitnesses were persecuted, tortured and put to death for their belief in the risen Christ—would you endure that to defend a lie?)

If I am wrong about my faith, I will still have lived a fulfilling, purposeful, hopeful life.

If unbelievers are wrong, they will spend eternity in unimaginable torment, completely separated from the goodness and love of God.

Who has the most to lose?

You see, it's not about whether we have faith, because we all do. It's about who or what we choose to put our faith in. I choose Jesus.

"That which was from the beginning, which we have heard, which we have seen with our eyes, which we have looked at and our hands have touched – this we proclaim concerning the Word of life. … We proclaim to you what we have seen and heard, so that you also may have fellowship with us. And our fellowship is with the Father and with His Son, Jesus Christ." – 1 John 1:1, 3

"And without faith it is impossible to please God, because anyone who comes to Him must believe that He exists and that He rewards those who earnestly seek Him." – Hebrews 11:6

<u>Let's Talk About Trusting God ... Group Discussion Questions</u>

1. Discuss this quote*: "When we depend upon organizations, we get what organizations can do; when we depend upon education, we get what education can do; when we depend upon man, we get what man can do; but when we depend upon prayer, we get what God can do." –* A.C. Dixon

2. Read Isaiah 31:1 – *"Woe to those who go down to Egypt for help and rely on horses, and trust in chariots because they are many and in horsemen because they are very strong, but they do not look to the Holy One of Israel, nor seek the LORD!"*

   - In Isaiah's day, God's people were tempted to trust in the strength of "horses, chariots and horsemen" to deliver them. What are some of the things we're tempted to trust, instead of God, in our day?

   - Have you ever trusted in something other than God and been disappointed?

3. Romans 10:17 says, *"So faith comes from hearing, and hearing by the word of Christ."* How is reading and studying God's Word related to our level of trust in Him?

4. Discuss some of the attributes of God, as given to us in the Bible, and how these attribute make it easier to trust Him.

5. Psalm 127:1 says, *"Unless the Lord builds the house, they labor in vain who build it; unless the Lord guards the city, the watchman keeps awake in vain."* With the message of this verse

in mind, finish the familiar phrases below and discuss whether or not each is biblical:

- "God helps those who help _____."
- "If you want something done right, you've got to _____ _____."
- "If I don't do it, it won't _____."

6. Read Proverbs 3:5-6 and discuss the following:

   - What does it mean to "not lean on your own understanding"?

   - Practically speaking, how do you acknowledge God in all your ways?

   - What does it mean that God "will make your paths straight"?

7. Read Matthew 18:1-4 and discuss how "becoming like children" relates to trusting God.

8. When we are praying for God to change something, it can be hard to trust His timing. Does knowing that He can suddenly change everything very quickly help you to continue to trust Him? Has God suddenly changed a difficult situation in your life?

9. What does it communicate to God when we trust Him? When we don't trust Him?

Dig a Little Deeper ... Individual Study

1. Is it hard for you to trust God? (Answer "yes," "no," or "it depends") _____

■ If you answered "yes," complete this sentence: It is hard for me to trust God because it is hard for me to believe _____

_____

_____

■ If you answered "no," complete this sentence: It is easy for me to trust God because _____

_____

_____

■ If you answered, "it depends," complete this sentence: I find it easy to trust God when _____

_____BUT difficult to trust Him when _____

_____

2. Read Matthew 18:1-4: *"At that time, the disciples came to Jesus and said, 'Who then is greatest in the kingdom of heaven?' And He called a child to Himself and set him before them, and said, 'Truly I say to you, unless you are converted and become like children, you will not enter the kingdom of heaven. Whoever then humbles himself as this child, he is the greatest in the kingdom of heaven.'"*

■ In what ways are children typically more trusting than adults?

_____

■ In what ways do you need to have a more childlike trust in the Lord? _____

_____

3. In Exodus 33:18, Moses asks God, *"I pray You, show me Your glory!"* In Exodus 34:6, we read, *"Then the LORD passed by in front of him (Moses) and proclaimed, 'The LORD, the LORD God, compassionate and gracious, slow to anger, and abounding in lovingkindness and truth ...'"*

   - Moses wanted to see the very essence of God (His glory), to know what He's really like. Underline the adjectives in the verse above (Exodus 34:6) that God used to describe Himself.

   - How do each of these character traits help you to trust God?

      - compassionate: _____

         _____

      - gracious: _____

         _____

      - slow to anger: _____

         _____

      - abounding in lovingkindness: _____

         _____

      - abounding in truth: _____

         _____

4. Read Philippians 4:19 – *"And my God will supply all your needs according to His riches in glory in Christ Jesus."*

   - How many of your needs does God promise to meet in this verse? _____

   - According to this verse, what kind of resources does God have to meet all your needs? _____

- If we define a need as something we cannot live without, what do you consider to be your needs? _____

  _____

  _____

  _____

- Pray through the list you made, placing each of your needs in God's hands.

5. Read 1 Chronicles 29:11-12 – *"'Yours, O Lord, is the greatness and the power and the glory and the victory and the majesty, indeed everything that is in the heavens and the earth; Yours is the dominion, O Lord, and You exalt Yourself as head over all. Both riches and honor come from You, and You rule over all, and in Your hand is power and might; and it lies in Your hand to make great and to strengthen everyone.'"*

- Is there anything in your world that does not belong to God or that He does not ultimately rule over_____

6. Read Jeremiah 32:17, 26 & 27 – *"'Ah Lord God! Behold, You have made the heavens and the earth by Your great power and by Your outstretched arm! Nothing is too difficult for You.... Then the word of the Lord came to Jeremiah, saying, 'Behold, I am the Lord, the God of all flesh; is anything too difficult for Me?'"*

- Is there anything in your life that you think is too difficult for God to do? Explain: _____

  _____

_____

_____

- If you answered "yes" above, do you really believe it is because this thing is too difficult for God, or is there another reason you find it hard to trust God to take care of it? _____

_____

_____

_____

_____

_____

7. Read Proverbs 3:5-6 – *"Trust in the Lord with all your heart and do not lean on your own understanding. In all your ways acknowledge Him, and He will make your paths straight."*

- Do you have a hard time not leaning on your own under-standing? Explain: _____

_____

_____

- What do you think it means to acknowledge God in all your ways? _____

_____

_____

- What are some of your strengths, gifts, talents and assets?

_____

_____

_____

- What are some of God's character traits, assets and abilities?

  _____

  _____

  _____

- Based on the previous two questions, whose credentials are more impressive—yours or God's? _____ Who is more trustworthy? _____

8. Read Isaiah 26:3: *"You will keep him in perfect peace, whose mind is stayed on You, because he trusts in You." (New King James Version)*

   - This verse implies that there is a cause-and-effect relationship between trusting God and what? _____

   - If we're trusting God, what will our minds be "stayed on"?

     _____

   - Rewrite this verse in your own words:_____

     _____

     _____

     _____

     _____

9. It's easy to grow weary as we trust God to change a difficult situation or person. We may be tempted to give up. That's when it can be very helpful to remember all the times in the Bible when God SUDDENLY changed someone's life—Moses, David, Mary, and the many people Jesus healed, for example. Has God

ever suddenly intervened and changed a difficult and seemingly hopeless situation in your life? Explain: _____

_____

_____

_____

_____

_____

_____

_____

10. Read the excerpt below from a sermon by John Piper (delivered 9-26-99 and reprinted on Piper's ministry website, www.desiringgod.com) and answer the question that follows it:

"Your daddy is standing in a swimming pool out a little bit from the edge. You are, let's say, three years old and standing on the edge of the pool. Daddy holds out his arms to you and says, 'Jump, I'll catch you. I promise.' Now, how do you make your daddy look good at that moment? Answer: trust him and jump. Have faith in him and jump. That makes him look strong and wise and loving. But if you won't jump, if you shake your head and run away from the edge, you make your daddy look bad. It looks like you are saying, 'he can't catch me' or 'he won't catch me' or 'it's not a good idea to do what he tells me to do.' And all three of those make your dad look bad. But you don't want to make God look bad. So you trust him. Then you make

him look good—which he really is. And that is what we mean when we say, 'Faith glorifies God' or 'Faith gives God glory.' It makes him look as good as He really is. So trusting God is really important."

- Does your level of trust in God make Him "look good" or "look bad"? _____

_____

_____

_____

_____

11. Finish this study with a time of prayer, confessing any trust issues you may have with God and reaffirming your willingness, desire and intention to trust Him more fully. You may use the lines below to write your prayer, if you wish:

_____

_____

_____

_____

_____

_____

_____

_____

_____

_____

*Do you picture God with His hands on His hips
and a frown on His face, growling,
"You got yourself into this, now you can get yourself out!"?
Guess what? He's not like that.
Let's talk about…*

REPENTANCE
& MERCY

Anything Bounced Off Your Truck?

Lost anything lately?

Everybody misplaces things from time to time. Car keys, T.V. remotes, reading glasses, pool tables. Well, okay, maybe not everybody loses pool tables, but I did one time and the story still boggles my mind.

My parents had generously given us money to buy a pool table for Christmas, so we shopped around and eventually ordered one from a store in a city about 60 miles away. When it came in, I hopped in our truck and went to pick it up.

The pool table was one of those "some-assembly-required" deals, so it came in two very large, heavy, flat boxes. The guys at the store helped me load it into my truck, assuring me that the boxes were so heavy that they could never fall out of the back, even though the tailgate had to be left down.

I trucked back to my house, thinking I would unload the boxes in the garage before picking up my sons at school. But when I got home, I discovered I couldn't hoist the heavy boxes out, so I got back in the truck and drove to the school. As I waited for my boys to come out, I got out of the truck, leaned against the tailgate, and began talking to a friend. A low-level warning signal began buzzing in my brain, but it took a few minutes for me to realize what was wrong..

I turned, glared at my EMPTY truck, and yelled, "OH NO! Where's my pool table?"

Predictably, my friend look confused and said, "Huh?"

"Please tell my boys I'll be right back," I said as I jumped in the cab of the truck and zoomed off in search of my lost boxes.

I frantically retraced my route from home to the school two times, in total disbelief that I could have driven 60 miles with those heavy boxes securely in the back, only to lose them somewhere in traffic in the middle of my town.

I didn't see the pool table on the side of the road anywhere, and I felt queasy as I imagined explaining this unexplainable situation to my kids, my husband and my parents. When I got home and dialed my husband's number at work, I felt like Lucy calling Ricky Ricardo (remember the *I Love Lucy* show?) to confess one of her zany mishaps.

Joe was as baffled as I was, and neither of us had any idea how to track down our lost pool table, so we decided we'd have to use some of our savings to replace it—or move to deepest, darkest Peru where my parents couldn't find us.

But, lo and behold, the next day we got a call from a supervisor with the city sanitation department. He told us that one of his work crews had seen the boxes bounce out of my truck into the street. These honest guys retrieved the boxes, which had our name and phone number on them, and turned them in to their supervisor.

The pool table was undamaged, but my state of mind? Not so much. I was left with many nagging questions about how I didn't notice those big boxes sliding out of my truck.

Life can be like that, too. We can lose things that are precious and not even realize they've slipped away until it seems too late. Our kids grow up and leave the nest, and we realize we never took time to really enjoy them; we look across the table at our spouse and discover that through selfish, mutual neglect, we hardly know the person we're married to; we let distractions and misplaced priorities dilute our faith so much that although we go to church, we live like atheists, going about life as though God doesn't exist.

Yes, important stuff can bounce out of our trucks and perhaps our only warning is an uncomfortable, low-level sense that something is off kilter.

Pay attention to those warnings. Take inventory. See what is gone or going, and talk to the One who can help you find it, repair it, restore it. Don't despair—Jesus said He came to seek and to save what is lost (Luke 19:10).

Bring on the Mercy!

Do you ever find yourself getting frustrated about your lot in life and thinking, "Hey, wait just a doggone minute–I deserve better than this! Just once I'd like to get what I deserve in life!"

Not me. I don't want what I deserve. I want grace and mercy.

Grace says, "You can't earn my love and blessings, but I'm going to give them to you anyway."

Mercy says, "You deserve punishment and wrath, but I'm choosing not to give you that."

So, yes, I most heartily say, "Please don't give me what I deserve, Lord. Bring on the grace and mercy!"

The other day, I was recalling a big slice of mercy I received one time. Just three weeks after buying a brand new car, I had an unfortunate encounter with the back end of another car at the post office. The other driver and I were both pulling out of parking spaces and sadly ended up on the same piece of pavement at precisely the same time. It wasn't pretty.

We decided we didn't need to call a police officer to the scene of our little mishap. We simply traded insurance info and went on our way. Weeks of hassles and phone calls followed and I was not optimistic that the situation could be resolved without costing me a significant wad of cash.

I replayed the fender-bender over and over in my brain, wishing that I'd hit a few more red lights on my way to the post office, or that the line had been a little slower—anything that might have kept me from pulling out of my parking spot exactly when I did.

When the whole accident mess was resolved, guess what? I didn't owe anybody any money! To this day, I'm not sure how that happened, but when you get a statement that says you don't owe any money, it's usually better not to ask questions. It's better to just be thankful. And I was. Boy howdy, I was. I thanked my insurance agent and God for delivering me out of the mess I had gotten myself into.

Can you relate? Have you ever been spared consequences you deserved? Often, we do reap what we sow, but every once in awhile, we don't. I spell that M-E-R-C-Y, and it's one of God's specialties.

There's a wonderful example of God's mercy in the book of Joshua. The Israelites were moving into the Promised Land and God told them not to make any peace treaties with the evil folks who lived there. But a sneaky group of Gibeonites tricked the children of Israel into signing a treaty with them.

A short time later, those rascally Gibeonites were attacked and they called upon their "covenant partners," the Israelites, to come to their rescue. God's people were caught between a rock and a hard place. They realized they had been tricked into this covenant, but they knew they were bound by it. And the Israelites weren't innocent—the Bible says they erred greatly when they signed the treaty without "inquiring of the Lord."

So, the Israelites had to help defend the Gibeonites. In fact, they had to march all night and then fight a tough battle that raged throughout the next day. Joshua and the Israelites needed some extra daylight to win the fight, so God came through with grade A miracle: He made the sun stand still long enough to give the Israeli army the victory.

That was mercy. The Israelites had gotten themselves into a jam through their own arrogance and impetuousness, but God didn't lean down from heaven and shout, "You got yourself into this, now you get yourselves out!" No, He had compassion on His children when they cried out to Him in humility and desperation.

He still does that today.

If you've blown it, humble yourself and cry out to Him. He can make the sun stand still if that's what is needed. He can even work in and through insurance companies to deliver His mercy to us. He sees; He knows; and He always acts for our good and His glory.

Psalm 28:6 – "Praise be to the LORD, for he has heard my cry for mercy."

"Bad Dog" and I Have a Lot in Common

If you don't read the newspaper from front page to back, you might miss some real gems. I recently got my biggest chuckle of the week from an advertisement tucked away in the classifieds.

Here's what it said: *"BAD DOG needs good home! Free 1.5-yr.-old female, spayed Boston terrier. Dislikes: obeying electric collars; being left alone; glowering, armed neighbors. Likes: kids; chasing cats; eating garbage; destroying holiday decorations. Call if you are patient and have a yard with an actual fence."*

After I got through laughing, I realized that this Boston terrier and I have a lot in common...

❖ I've never worn an electric dog collar (although my parents may have considered it when I was a teenager), but I'm sure I wouldn't like it. Nobody likes to be told they can't do something they want to do or go someplace they want to go.

❖ It's stupid to violate the loving boundaries God sets, but that doesn't mean I don't sometimes try. No electric shock collars for God's children, though—the Holy Spirit knows how to give us a jolt when we're heading out of bounds.

❖ Like this Boston terrier, I don't like being left alone. As exasperating as people can sometimes be, I'd hate to do life all by myself. And living without God's good and loving presence is a scary proposition, for sure, and one that thankfully, His children never have to experience. "I will never desert you, nor will I ever forsake you," He promises. (Hebrews 13:5)

❖ I don't like "glowering, armed neighbors," either. Fortunately, I don't have any, but I do occasionally bump up against folks who've had all the warm and fuzzy parts of their personalities worn off. I've also been on the receiving end of a "glower" (a resentful stare). It's never fun to wonder if you're about to become a crime statistic.

❖ Dogs who like kids can't be all bad, right? I like kids, too. They are typically honest, forgiving and quick to laugh, and in that sense, wonderful role models for us all.

❖ The ad said my Boston terrier soulmate likes to chase cats and eat garbage. I don't chase cats, unless they are stinking up my porch, but if eating garbage includes Twizzlers and cookies, then I guess I'm guilty.

I checked the newspaper a few days after I first saw the ad and couldn't find it. I suspect and hope that someone was as charmed by the description as I was and adopted that pup.

So, who would adopt a "bad dog" with so many irritating habits and vices?

More importantly, who would adopt me ... or you ... with all our weaknesses, bad habits and sins?

God would. And He does, if we accept His adoption plan—the gift of salvation He offers through Jesus. The magic of Christmas is the incomprehensible wonder of a holy God passionately desiring to embrace unholy people like you and me, crediting to our bankrupt accounts the righteousness of Jesus, and bringing us home to His heart.

"But God demonstrates His own love toward us, in that while we were still sinners, Christ died for us." (Romans 5:8)

"He predestined us to adoption as sons through Jesus Christ to Himself, according to the kind intention of His will..." (Ephesians 1:5)

Let's Talk About Repentance & Mercy ... Group Discussion Questions

1. What prevents us from sometimes realizing that important things are slipping from our lives?

2. What are some common regrets people have as they look back over their lives?

3. How should we, as Christians, deal with the feelings of shame, condemnation and guilt that come when we realize we have made mistakes or gotten our priorities out of order?

4. A popular Christian song says the slide into sin for a Christian is a "slow fade." What do you think this means? Have you experienced a "slow fade" in your life or observed it in the lives of other Christians?

5. Sometimes we don't realize we are drifting from God's path, so God uses others as agents of His mercy to help us see our folly. Read Matthew 18:15 and Galatians 6:1. Why are we usually so reluctant to actually do what these verses command us to do?

6. It's easy to let relationships fall into disrepair, especially our relationship with God. In what ways do Christians sometimes actually live like atheists—as though God doesn't even exist? If we find ourselves doing that, how can we fix it?

7. Read Isaiah 1:18, Joel 2:12-13, and Luke 15:18-20 and discuss this question: What is God's response when we return and recommit ourselves to Him?

8. If you got what you deserved, do you think your life would be better or worse?

9. How would you respond to someone who says, "I've drifted so far from God that there is no going back. He could never love me—I've done too many bad things."?

Dig a Little Deeper … Individual Study

1. Take an inventory of your life and consider this question: Are there good things you may have let "slip off your truck"? Explain: _____

   _____

   _____

   _____

   _____

2. Write a want ad, like the one quoted in the story about the "bad dog," describing yourself (no cheating allowed—be honest about your strengths and weaknesses): _____

   _____

   _____

   _____

   _____

   - In light of what you wrote above, do you find it easy or difficult to wrap your brain and heart around the truth that

God wants to be merciful to you and adopt you as His own? Explain: _____

_____

_____

_____

3. Can you describe any times when you received mercy instead of the judgment and punishment you deserved? _____

_____

_____

_____

_____

_____

4. God frequently had to discipline the nation of Israel when they wandered from His will. Sometimes that discipline came in the form of enemies who invaded and conquered the Israelites, but God's heart was always to restore His people to Himself ... and it still is. Read this verse and answer the questions below:

Joel 2:12-13, 25: "'Yet even now,' declares the LORD, 'Return to Me with all your heart, and with fasting, weeping and mourning; and rend your heart and not your garments.' Now return to the LORD your God, for He is gracious and compassionate, slow to anger, abounding in lovingkindness and relenting of evil. ... 'Then I will make up to you for the years that the swarming locust has eaten, The creeping locust, the stripping locust and the gnawing locust, my great army which I sent among you.'"

- Does it feel like "swarming locusts" have in some ways devoured pieces of your life, as a result of any rebellion against God? Explain: _____

  _____

  _____

- What do these verses in Joel promise to those who return to the Lord for a fresh start?

  _____

  _____

5. Haggai 1:5-7 says, *"Now therefore, thus says the LORD of hosts,'Consider your ways! You have sown much, but harvest little; you eat, but there is not enough to be satisfied; you drink, but there is not enough to become drunk; you put on clothing, but no one is warm enough; and he who earns, earns wages to put into a purse with holes.' Thus says the LORD of hosts, 'Consider your ways!'"*

- Take a few moments now to "consider your ways." If you are completely honest, are there lifestyle changes you could make that might help preserve or restore those things that are truly important in your life? Explain _____

  _____

  _____

  _____

6. Sometimes sin—our own or the sin of others against us—robs us of things that are truly important to us. Psalm 51 is a prayer of King David after he was confronted with his sins of adultery and murder, resulting from his illicit relationship with Bathsheba. In Psalm 51:12, David prays, *"Restore to me the joy of Your salvation and sustain me with a willing spirit."* Are there sins you have committed, or sins that were committed against you, that have robbed you of joy or peace? Explain: _____

_____

_____

_____

_____

_____

_____

7. Write the action(s) we are told to take in the following verses:

  ▪ 1 John 1:9 – *"If we confess our sins, He is faithful and righteous to forgive us our sins and to cleanse us from all unrighteousness."* _____

  ▪ Psalm 62:8 – *"Trust in Him at all times, O people; pour out your heart before Him; God is a refuge for us."* _____

  _____

  ▪ Ephesians 4:31-32 – *"Let all bitterness and wrath and anger and clamor and slander be put away from you, along with all malice. Be kind to one another, tenderhearted, forgiving each other, just as God in Christ also has forgiven you."* _____

_____

_____

_____

- The first two verses address your relationship with _____; the third verse addresses how you relate to _____ .

- When we realize we have sinned, why is it important to deal with our relationship with God and, in some cases, with other people? _____

_____

8. Look at 1 John 1:9 again – *"If we confess our sins, He is faithful and righteous to forgive us our sins and to cleanse us from all unrighteousness."*

- To "confess" essentially means to say the same thing about your sin that God says about it. According to 1 John 1:9, what will God do if you confess your sin? _____

- Why do we ever hesitate to confess our sins to Him? _____

_____

_____

9. In Luke 15, Jesus told a story we commonly call the "Parable of the Prodigal Son." There are several important lessons and truths to be gleaned from this story, one of which is God's heart toward a repentant sinner who returns to Him. In Luke 15:20, we see the Father's reaction when the prodigal son finally returns home: *"...So he got up and came to his father. But while he was*

still a long way off, his father saw him and felt compassion for him, and ran and embraced him and kissed him."

- How do you suppose the father was able to see the son while the son was still a long way off? _____

   _____

- What did the Father feel for the son? _____

- What did the Father do to express his feelings for his son?

   _____

10. Read Luke 15:22-24—*"But the father said to his slaves, 'Quickly bring out the best robe and put it on him, and put a ring on his hand and sandals on his feet; and bring the fattened calf, kill it, and let us eat and celebrate; for this son of mine was dead and has come to life again; he was lost and has been found.' And they began to celebrate."*

- Is it hard for you to imagine God throwing a party for you if you have blown it, repented and then returned for forgiveness? Why or why not? _____

   _____

   _____

   _____

   _____

   _____

   _____

11. Complete the two sentences below:

   ▪ In the past, if I've sinned and gone to God to ask for forgiveness, I usually felt like He _____

   _____

   _____

   _____

   ▪ According to what I've learned in this study, from now on, if I sin and go to God to ask for forgiveness, I believe that He will

   _____

   _____

   _____

   _____

12. If your own sin has robbed you of joy or peace, confess those sins to God right now and receive His forgiveness and restoration. If the sins of others against you have stolen your joy or peace, pour out your heart to God in prayer and ask Him to help you forgive those who have hurt you and to restore your joy and peace. And remember, forgiveness doesn't make the other person right; it just makes you free. Space is provided below if you'd like to write out your prayer:

   _____

   _____

   _____

   _____

   _____

We don't deserve it. We can't comprehend it.
We're not always very good at accepting it
or passing it on.
And yet God continues to give it lavishly and
unconditionally.
Let's talk about …

GOD'S LOVE

God Loves Us, Wrinkles and All

You've probably heard the admonition, "Be careful what you ask for." Well, put that together with another old adage about "learning things the hard way," and you've got a picture of my life with Winston the Psycho Pup.

Winston was a Christmas present—a most thoughtful, loving present from my husband. He—Winston, not my husband—is a shar-pei, the adorable, oft-photographed dogs whose skin is ten times bigger than their frames—a trait I can relate to. Winston is the third shar-pei we've owned, but nothing like his predecessors, or any others of his breed that I've read about.

Dog books describe shar-peis as distant, aloof and "of regal bearing." Winston obviously never read these books. Thus far, this gift that keeps on giving has only two speeds: wide open and asleep.

Our other shar-peis liked to be held as pups and it was sheer bliss to snuggle with those little bags 'o wrinkles. Winston, on the other hand, does not cuddle. Winston cavorts. Winston conquers. But Winston does not cuddle. To him, life is one big romp and all the world's a chew toy. When we let him outside, Winston shoots out the door like a cannonball and runs as fast as he can around our wooded acreage. He runs and runs and runs and never seems to get tired. The Forest Gump of dogs.

Winston wasn't neutered before we got him, but we're beginning to wonder if he had a doggy lobotomy. When he looks up at me with his slightly cross-eyed, goofy gaze, I have to consider the real possibility that he is not dealing with a full deck.

Early on, Joe began to wonder if bringing this Tasmanian-devil dog into our home might have been a big mistake. He even considered shipping Winston to another port, but my feeling was that SOMEONE needed to love Winston and it was apparently our calling.

Now, don't get me wrong. Winston is cute. Real cute. It's possibly his sole redeeming quality at this point. When he goes to sleep, lays his jaws on his paws and spreads out across the floor like a glorious puddle of skin, it is nearly more cuteness than a soul can bear.

One thing I forgot to mention—Winston was expensive. Joe had to shell out some significant bucks to purchase this little piece of insanity for me. That alone is enough to keep me committed to Winston, but I also cling to the belief that he will eventually become a far better dog than he is right now.

When Winston drives me to the brink of total exasperation, I remember that Someone had to pay a lot for me once, too. Infinitely more than we paid for our dog. God had to give His Son, Jesus, to ransom my life and adopt me into His family. And while we didn't quite know what we were getting with Winston, God knew exactly what He was getting when He got me ... and He adopted me anyway.

Some days, it probably seems like my elevator doesn't quite make it to the top floor, either. Sometimes I get a little hyper and act a little nuts. I've been known to jump, bite, bark, whine and chase when I shouldn't. I can be high maintenance.

We're looking forward to the day when Winston will cease to be the "be-careful-what-you-ask-for" dog and become the "so-thankful-for-what-you-have" dog. Until that time, we will love him anyway. Why? Because he is ours.

And when I look at him, I'll remember a Heavenly Father who loves me that way, too, wrinkles and all.

The Heart of a Grandparent

Lots of cuteness, cuddling and fun, without the intense stress of parenthood. Yes, indeed, I am thoroughly loving this grandma gig.

Now I completely understand the bumper sticker that says, "If I'd known grandchildren were this much fun, I'd have had them first!"

I clearly remember how stressed out I got when my sons were babies and occasionally launched into crying jags. I wanted to move heaven and earth to fix whatever was wrong. Their cries were like a call to arms, a shrieking fire alarm, a tornado warning, a medical "code blue." Their distress made me feel like a giant gorilla was jumping up and down on my heart and screaming, "Fix it ... fix it ... FIX it!"

But sometimes, I just didn't know how.

I changed diapers, I fed, I burped, I rocked, I sang, I kissed, I held, and I soothed. I did the best I could, but I was always, always keenly aware that I was not doing any of it perfectly. The immense implications—real and imagined—of my parenting performance weighed heavily upon me.

Older women said to me, "This time goes by so quickly; be sure you enjoy your children when they are young."

I did enjoy my kids ... a lot. And I loved them always, but there were times when being a new parent was too overwhelming to be a barrel of laughs. The years flew by, but sometimes the days and nights seemed to last forever.

But being a grandma isn't like that. The years grace grandparents with more patience, perspective, and permission to allow our children to rightfully take on the tougher responsibilities of childrearing.

While our kids gnaw on the sometimes gristly meat of parenthood, we grandparents get to enjoy the dessert.

So Edda Rose and Walter, the little desserts I've thus far been blessed to relish, I'm serving notice to you, and to all the others God may graciously send, that I plan to fully exercise my right to love you, spoil you, enjoy you, and giggle with you over stuff parents sometimes don't feel permission to giggle about.

I've earned my "Gram" badge and I plan to wear it.

And I will forever be grateful to you for reminding me how God loves me. For reminding me that His love isn't just a serious, heavy, take-your-medicine love. It's also a playful, delightful, throw-your-head-back-and-laugh love.

You have reminded me of something God said to and about His children: *"The Lord your God is with you, He is mighty to save. He will take great delight in you, He will quiet you with his love, He will rejoice over you with singing." (Zephaniah 3:17)*

His is the heart of a perfect parent AND a perfect grandparent. It's easy for me to forget that God takes great delight in me, that He rejoices over me with singing. And then you remind me. You charge toward me and jump with abandon into my arms. I sweep you up and you lay your head on my shoulder.

And I am reminded that this is what my heavenly Father wants most from me. This is what delights His heart. This is how He feels about me.

And you inspire me to run to Him.

A Diamond or a Truck?

I recently saw a billboard that has now earned a spot on my best-ever list. Advertising a jewelry store, the sign read: *"If she said she wanted an engagement truck, would you hesitate?"*

Talk about getting to the heart of a matter.

It got me thinking about how my husband might react if I ever told him I really, really wanted a truck. Or a tractor. Or some kind of power tool.

After he regained consciousness, I'm pretty sure we'd be on our way lickety-split to a hardware store, truck dealership, or farm equipment place.

While that scene is seriously unlikely to ever actually happen, I have, in the past, offhandedly mentioned that perhaps a new computer, or an IPOD, or a high-def T.V. might be nice. Whew buddy, my husband was all over those barely whispered hints like white on rice.

On the other hand, requests for new furniture, carpet or wallpaper generally fall on slightly ... um ... shall we say, less eager ears.

Here's my best guess at how a guy brain processes such requests ...

"What's wrong with our furniture? I don't see springs poking out anywhere and a little duct tape will keep that stuffing from coming out."

"New wallpaper? Our walls have paper on them?"

"We don't need new carpet. Some of this carpet still looks as good as new. Move that couch and I'll show you. Bet we can get another 20 years out of this if we just rearrange the furniture."

So, you see, when the first step toward marital bliss involves spending money on something as hugely impractical as a diamond engagement ring, it's more than some guys can handle. Maybe more men would head for the altar if women would opt instead for engagement trucks, engagement bass boats, or engagement big-screen T.V.s.

Might be something to think about, all you single gals out there. Or not.

The truth is, we all want to be loved extravagantly. We want to know we're worth a gift that comes wrapped in sacrificial, unselfish love. Great love is worthy of grand, extravagant expressions.

God knows all about that. After all, *"God so loved the world that He gave His one and only Son ..."* (John 3:16)

Go ahead—insert your name in there where it says "the world." God gave His Son for you.

Extravagant. Unselfish. An unimaginable sacrifice.

How should we respond to so great a gift, so great a love? With grand gestures of thankfulness.

The Gospel of Mark (chapter 14) tells us about a woman who showed up at a dinner party and anointed the head of Jesus with an incredibly expensive jar of perfume. Rebuked by some bystanders for her "wastefulness," Jesus defended her, saying her extravagant expression of devotion would be told throughout the world. And so it was.

We should respond to God's love for us by giving Him that which most delights His heart—our hearts, our lives.

If He said He simply wanted us to go to church on Christmas and Easter and toss a few bucks in the offering plate, would we hesitate?

Probably not. That's easy.

But if He's worthy at all, He's worthy of all.

"What shall I render to the LORD for all His benefits toward me? I shall lift up the cup of salvation and call upon the name of the LORD.—Psalm 116:12-13

Let's Talk About God's Love ... Group Discussion Questions

1. Do you usually feel like God's love for you is dependent upon your performance and behavior? If so, how do you ever know if you're worthy or unworthy of God's love? Read Romans 5:8, Romans 8:1, and Ephesians 2:4-7 and discuss how these verses address this question.

2. When you do something you know is wrong, do you ever shy away from God (or other Christians) because you feel like God is mad at you? How might that be counter-productive and even dangerous?

3. Does God's unconditional love motivate you to be more or less obedient to Him?

4. Read 1 Corinthians 6:20. If you save and plan and finally get to buy something you've wanted for a long time, how do you feel about it when you bring it home? Is it hard for you to believe that God feels that way about you?

5. What is the difference between the love of a parent for a child and the love of a grandparent for a grandchild? How is God's love for us a perfect version of both of those loves?

6. Although God's love is unconditional and unchanging, regardless of our response to it, what response do you think probably blesses Him the most?

7. What are some examples of half-hearted, token gestures we can be guilty of offering to God in response to His love? Discuss this phrase: "If He is worthy at all, He is worthy of all."

8. Read Ephesians 3:17-19. Why is it so vital for Christians to know they are loved by God?

Dig a Little Deeper ... Individual Study

1. What's your immediate response when you read that God's love is unending, unchanging and unconditional—in other words, that it doesn't depend upon your behavior or performance? ___

   _____

   _____

   _____

   _____

   _____

2. Do you ever think, "If people knew what I was really like inside, there's no way they would love me"? _____

   _____

   - If you answered "yes" to that question, why do you feel this way? _____

     _____

     _____

     _____

3. Think about the person who knows you better than anyone else in this world. Are there still things they don't know about you?

_____

4. Read the verses below and answer the questions that follow:

- Jeremiah 1:5: *"'Before I formed you in the womb I knew you, and before you were born I consecrated you; I have appointed you a prophet to the nations.'"*

- Psalm 139:1-4, 15-16: *"O LORD, You have searched me and known me. You know when I sit down and when I rise up; You understand my thought from afar. You scrutinize my path and my lying down, and are intimately acquainted with all my ways. Even before there is a word on my tongue, Behold, O LORD, You know it all. ... My frame was not hidden from You, when I was made in secret, and skillfully wrought in the depths of the earth; Your eyes have seen my unformed substance; and in Your book were all written the days that were ordained for me, when as yet there was not one of them."*

- Do these verses indicate that God knows everything about you? _____

- What are the first words that come to your mind when you realize that God knows everything about you, and always has? _____

_____

_____

5. Read the verses below and answer the question that follows:

- Romans 5:8 – *"But God demonstrates His own love toward us, in that while we were yet sinners, Christ died for us."*

- Titus 3:5-7 – *"He saved us, not on the basis of deeds which we have done in righteousness, but according to His mercy, by the washing of regeneration and renewing by the Holy Spirit, whom He poured out upon us richly through Jesus Christ our Savior, so that being justified by His grace we would be made heirs according to the hope of eternal life."*

- Ephesians 2:8-9 – *"For by grace you have been saved through faith; and that not of yourselves, it is the gift of God; not as a result of works, so that no one may boast."*

- Summarize how these verses refute this lie: "God can't love me. I'm not good enough to be His child.": _____

  _____

  _____

  _____

  _____

  _____

  _____

6. Redemption means to buy, get or win something (or someone) back, or to set something (or someone) free from captivity.

- In light of this definition, what does it mean that Jesus came to redeem you and me? _____

  _____

_____

_____

7. Read the verses below and answer the questions that follow:

  ▪ 1 Corinthians 6:20a says this: *"For you have been bought with a price …"*

  ▪ John 3:16 – *"For God so loved the world, that He gave His only begotten Son, that whoever believes in Him shall not perish, but have eternal life."*

  ▪ Colossians 1:12-14 – *"…giving thanks to the Father, who has qualified us to share in the inheritance of the saints in Light. For He rescued us from the domain of darkness, and trans-ferred us to the kingdom of His beloved Son, in whom we have redemption, the forgiveness of sins."*

  ▪ What price did God pay for you? _____

  ▪ Why did God pay so much for you? _____

  ▪ Insert your name in the blanks: For God so loved _____

    _____, that He gave His only begotten Son, that

    _____ shall not perish, but have eternal life.

  ▪ When God "bought" you, what were you rescued from? ___

  _____

  _____

  _____

  ▪ If you buy something very expensive, how do you feel about it and care for it when you take it home? _____

  _____

- Stop for a moment now and try to absorb the truth that God ransomed and redeemed you with the blood of His Son, Jesus. Express your thoughts about that here: _____

  _____

  _____

  _____

  _____

  _____

8. Read the words of Jesus in John 10:11-15 and answer the questions that follow: *"I am the good shepherd; the good shepherd lays down His life for the sheep. He who is a hired hand, and not a shepherd, who is not the owner of the sheep, sees the wolf coming, and leaves the sheep and flees, and the wolf snatches them and scatters them. He flees because he is a hired hand and is not concerned about the sheep. I am the good shepherd, and I know My own and My own know Me, even as the Father knows Me and I know the Father; and I lay down My life for the sheep."*

   - Tending sheep was a common occupation in the time of Jesus. How do you think a good shepherd felt about his sheep? ____

     _____

     _____

   - What kinds of things would a good shepherd do to care for his sheep?_____

     _____

- What might a bad shepherd or hired hand do to his sheep?

  _____

  _____

  _____

- Summarize what Jesus is saying to you when He says you are His sheep and He is the Good Shepherd: _____

  _____

  _____

  _____

  _____

9. Read Romans 8:15 – "*For you have not received a spirit of slavery leading to fear again, but you have received a spirit of adoption as sons by which we cry out, "'Abba! Father!'"*

   - "Abba" is a Hebrew word that is comparable to "Daddy" in English—one of the most familiar, endearing names a child calls his or her father. Does it make you uncomfortable to think of addressing God as "Daddy"? _____ Explain why or why not: _____

     _____

     _____

     _____

     _____

   - What are the differences between being a slave and being a son? _____

_____

_____

- Do you usually feel more like God's slave or His beloved child? _____

_____

_____

_____

10. When we are in the midst of difficult, painful or even tragic circumstances, we can feel like God is not a perfect father or a good shepherd. Are there times when a parent or a shepherd has to stand by and allow those under his care to go through painful things? _____

_____

_____

_____

11. Read the words of Jesus in John 13:34-35 – "'A new commandment I give to you, that you love one another, even as I have loved you, that you also love one another. By this all men will know that you are My disciples, if you have love for one another.'"

- Jesus said we are to love one another "even as" He has loved us. What are some adjectives you would use to describe the love Jesus has for you? _____

_____

- How would you rate yourself when it comes to loving others "even as" Jesus loves you? _____

  _____

  _____

- Can you identify any practical ways you could better love the people in your life? _____

  _____

  _____

  _____

12. Read Psalm 116:12-13 – *"What shall I render to the LORD for all His benefits toward me? I shall lift up the cup of salvation and call upon the name of the LORD."*

    - "Lifting up the cup of salvation" includes remembering and rejoicing in the gift of salvation we've received through Jesus Christ and celebrating the eternal life He offers us. "Calling upon the name of the Lord" includes proclaiming His name, as well as crying out to Him for His help and provision. Psalm 116 indicates that these are appropriate responses to God's "benefits"—His blessings and love.

    - Explain in your own words how you can honor, bless and thank God by "lifting up the cup of salvation" and "calling upon the name of the Lord": _____

      _____

      _____

      _____

_____

_____

_____

- Sometimes we offer half-hearted, token gestures to God in response to His love. What are some examples of these? ____

_____

_____

_____

- Explain what you think this phrase means: "If He is worthy at all, He is worthy of all."

_____

_____

_____

_____

_____

13. In Ephesians 3:1, we read a prayer of the Apostle Paul for the church at Ephesus. Here is part of that prayer (verses 17b-19): *"...that you, being rooted and grounded in love, may be able to comprehend with all the saints what is the breadth and length and height and depth, and to know the love of Christ which surpasses knowledge, that you may be filled up to all the fullness of God."* Write out a prayer for yourself based on these verses:

_____

_____

_____